GLUTEN-FREE KIDS LUNCH BREAK

60 FUSS-FREE DELICIOUS, EASY-TO-MAKE, SCHOOL-READY BREAKFAST, SNACK, & LUNCH RECIPES

EVA ILIANA

© Copyright 2020 - **All rights reserved.**

The content contained within this book may not be reproduced, duplicated or transmitted without direct written permission from the author or the publisher.

Under no circumstances will any blame or legal responsibility be held against the publisher, or author, for any damages, reparation, or monetary loss due to the information contained within this book, either directly or indirectly.

Legal Notice:

This book is copyright protected. It is only for personal use. You cannot amend, distribute, sell, use, quote or paraphrase any part, or the content within this book, without the consent of the author or publisher.

Disclaimer Notice:

Please note the information contained within this document is for educational and entertainment purposes only. All effort has been executed to present accurate, up to date, reliable, complete information. No warranties of any kind are declared or implied. Readers acknowledge that the author is not engaged in the rendering of legal, financial, medical or professional advice. The content within this book has been derived from various sources. Please consult a licensed professional before attempting any techniques outlined in this book.

By reading this document, the reader agrees that under no circumstances is the author responsible for any losses, direct or indirect, that are incurred as a result of the use of the information contained within this document, including, but not limited to, errors, omissions, or inaccuracies.

CONTENTS

Introduction: Going Gluten-Free — 7

1. ALL ABOUT CELIAC DISEASE — 13
   - Understanding Celiac Disease — 13
   - Did You Know? Interesting Facts About Celiac Disease — 16
   - Dealing with Celiac Disease — 21
   - Understanding Other Auto-Immune Disorders — 24
   - Enter, Gluten — 29
   - When Celiac Disease and Gluten Meet — 31
   - The Wonders of Going Gluten-Free — 34

2. THE PROS AND CONS OF A GLUTEN-FREE DIET — 37
   - The Gluten-Free Craze — 38
   - Is Your Child Gluten-Intolerant? — 41
   - Going Gluten-Free: A Choice or a Requirement? — 45
   - Health Benefits of the Gluten-Free Diet — 46
   - The Potential Downsides You Should Know About — 52
   - Other Treatments for Celiac Disease — 56

3. EMPOWERING YOUR CHILD TO CHOOSE HEALTH — 59
   - The Gluten-Free Diet for Children — 60
   - How Does the Gluten-Free Diet Help Children? — 62
   - The Rise of Gluten-Free Food — 67

Go Shopping With Your Child	68
Promote the Diet Through Social Media	72
Help Your Child Transition to the Gluten-Free Diet	77
Empower Your Child for the Future	83

4. BREAKFAST RECIPES FOR THE WIN! 88
   - The Most Important Meal of the Day 89
   - Try Not to Overdo It! 90
   - Sweet Potato Smoothie Bowl 92
   - Power Breakfast Bowl 94
   - Savory Crepes 95
   - Cinnamon Toast Breakfast Muffins 97
   - Morning Mac & Cheese 99
   - Classic Blueberry Muffins 102
   - Mediterranean Quiches 104
   - Cookies for Breakfast! 107
   - Savory Oat Bowl 109
   - Chocolate Chip Pancakes With Oats 111
   - Good Morning Burrito 113
   - Super-Powered Chia Pudding 115
   - Sweet Potato French Toast 117
   - Brekkie Pizza 119
   - Peanut Butter Pancakes 121
   - Italian Bake 123
   - Classic Oatmeal With Caramelized Banana 125
   - Breakfast Salad With Grilled Fruits 127
   - Coco-Banana Waffles 129
   - Eggy Breakfast Cups 132

5. SNACKING LIKE A BOSS 134
   - The Importance of Snacks 134
   - Snacking Wisely vs. Snacking Mindlessly 136
   - Classic Corn Dogs 139

Guilt-Free Chocolate Pudding	142
Sweet Potato Shoestring Fries	143
Mini Candy Corn Muffins	145
Quinoa Veggie Bites	148
Sweet and Healthy Parfaits	149
Healthy Homemade Chips	151
Crispy Granola Bars	152
Cauliflower Tots	154
Graham Crackers	156
Baked Mozzarella Sticks	158
Pumpkin Brownie Bars	160
Pillow-Soft Mini Pretzels	163
Fruit Platter With Sweet Hummus Dip	166
Tasty Pizza Bites	167
Sticky Chia Pudding	169
Pizza With Orange Sauce	171
Bagel Chips With Raisins and Cinnamon	174
Cheesy Baked Crisps	176
Frozen Protein Bars	177
6. LUNCH IDEAS THAT WILL MAKE YOUR CHILD'S FRIENDS JEALOUS	180
Having Lunch at School	181
Lunch is an Important Meal, Too	184
Fresh Lettuce Wraps	185
Fish and Veggie Sticks	187
Rainbow Rice Bowl	190
BLT Lunchbox	192
Grilled Turkey Kabobs	193
Chicken Cauli-Rice Bowl	196
Classic Spaghetti and Ground Meatballs	198
Deconstructed Fish Tacos	200
Build Your Own Egg Cups	202

Steak and Eggs Salad	203
Beef Tacos With Avocado	205
Broiled Chicken Drumsticks	207
Stuffed Avocado Boats	209
Cuban-Style Picadillo	211
Grain-Free Lunch Wraps	212
Skillet Shrimp With Feta	214
Hearty Vegetable Soup	216
Grilled Pork Chops	218
Thai-Style Noodle Soup Bowl	220
Skillet Chili	223
Conclusion: Healthy, Gluten-Free Recipes for Your Child	225
References	229

INTRODUCTION: GOING GLUTEN-FREE

"Being Celiac turned my life around for the better. I care about what I eat. I am fit, my body is in the best shape it's ever been. Crazy that Celiac is what opened my eyes."

— (UNKNOWN)

INTRODUCTION: GOING GLUTEN-FREE

As a parent, you always want to make sure that your children are healthy, happy, and strong. While there are many challenges that come with raising a family, things get even more complicated when you discover that your child has celiac disease. With this disease, you have to be very careful about what to feed your child.

Fortunately, this resource will provide you with all the information you need to ensure that your child's diet is healthy, safe, and enjoyable. Although many wonder about the cause of celiac disease, nobody has figured out an exact cause yet. However, it does seem like this disease tends to run in families. This means that if your child has celiac disease, there is a very high likelihood that someone else in your family has it, too. In the U.S. alone, around 1 in every 133 people suffers from this disease. In some cases, people who suffer from celiac disease don't even know they have it. If you're reading this, it means that you already know that your child has celiac disease. The great thing is that you want to do something about it like learn more about the disease and what you can do to help your child out.

Typically, when a child suffers from celiac disease, even the smallest amount of gluten can cause a lot of adverse effects. Gluten triggers their body to release antibodies, which quickly start attacking their system. The attacks are mainly centered on the child's intestines, which is why they have trouble with nutrient absorption. Naturally, this leads to a lack of nutrients, which they need to thrive. Aside from this main effect, gluten may also cause bloating, gas, or diarrhea. Some children who suffer from celiac disease may either lose or gain weight, but not in a healthy way. When the condition is left untreated or unchecked, it might lead to other health issues like osteoporosis, anemia, and neurological disorders. This is why it's so important to learn how to help your child manage their diagnosis.

There is another condition known as Non-Celiac Gluten Sensitivity (NCGS), and it's symptoms are similar to celiac disease. But the main difference is that children don't experience reactions as severe as those who suffer from celiac disease. Either way, it's best to have your child checked to make sure. It is also important to consult with your child's doctor regularly if they suffer from celiac disease, since your child's diet isn't the only thing you have to keep track of.

At this point, you might be wondering why I have so much to share about celiac disease. The reason for this is that I have been suffering from this crippling condition for more than five years now. I am now in my mid-30s, and this condition has taught me so much. When I first found out that I had developed celiac disease, I learned everything I could about it.

INTRODUCTION: GOING GLUTEN-FREE

The truth is, going gluten-free was never in my plans. While I had heard about gluten-free diets, I wasn't really interested in them. Sometimes, though, life throws us a curveball that will force us onto a new path. For me, that curveball was celiac disease. The first time I experienced the symptoms of this disease, I didn't give them much thought. Whenever I got stomach aches, gas, or even diarrhea, I always blamed these symptoms on the last thing I ate. But then I started seeing a pattern—I always experienced symptoms whenever I ate cereals, bread, cakes, pasta, and other high-gluten foods. To put my mind at ease, I consulted with a doctor, and that was when I was officially diagnosed with celiac disease.

That was more than five years ago. Since then, I have educated myself on my condition, how it affects the human body, and how I can **better manage it**. One of the most effective ways is by following a gluten-free diet. For the past five years, **I have experienced** cooking my own food, as well. After a few months, I realized that going gluten-free was one of the best decisions I have ever made in my life. Even though originally, it wasn't really my choice. Now, I wish that I had made this decision earlier—even before I developed celiac disease.

As someone who developed celiac disease as an adult, this is one realization that I want other people to have. I want to

INTRODUCTION: GOING GLUTEN-FREE

help you make the right decisions faster, especially while your child is still young. By helping your child transition to a gluten-free diet as early as possible, you can empower them to lead a healthier **lifestyle** without feeling defeated by a disease. Since I am someone who follows the gluten-free diet as part of my lifestyle, I have a passion for helping others learn more about it.

I also happen to be a mother of two beautiful children whom I have helped transition into this diet. Personally, I have seen firsthand how the gluten-free diet changed their lives, as well. By the end of this book, I promise that you will have a better understanding of what the gluten-free diet is all about, how it will benefit your child (and yourself, if you decide to make the change with them), and how to help your child go gluten-free. I have written this book because I believe that humanity will be better off without gluten in our diets. I want to see a future of truly healthy and energized adults who don't see their diets **as being a** "struggle."

Whether your child suffers from celiac disease, NCGS, or is completely healthy, the gluten-free diet is beneficial. But, if your child does suffer from this condition, **then this diet** is essential as part of their treatment. Of course, the gluten-free diet is a specialized one, which means that you have to learn how to follow it properly so that you don't compromise your child's health—and that is where this book comes in. If you're ready to learn all about going gluten-free with kids, **along with discovering** several amazing recipes, let's begin!

1

ALL ABOUT CELIAC DISEASE

Before we can move on to understanding the impact of celiac disease on the life of your child, you must first understand what this condition is all about. In this chapter, we will focus on the science of celiac disease to help you learn how it **operates and what happens** inside the body of those **suffering** from it. We will also discuss the evolutionary and biological line of gluten and how we **have come to live with it**. By the end of this chapter, you will have a better idea of what celiac disease is all about, which will make it easier for you to help your child.

UNDERSTANDING CELIAC DISEASE

Celiac disease is a type of autoimmune disease that is categorized as 'serious.' People from all over the world suffer from this disease, but the level of severity may vary from one person to another. When a person with celiac disease eats food that contains gluten, their body's immune system responds by attacking the small intestine. Over time, these attacks cause damage to the small intestine, which, in turn, leads to a reduced ability to properly absorb nutrients. Naturally, if this happens in young children, it will cause a lot of issues with their growth and development.

Celiac disease affects 1 in every 100 people around the world and it is believed to be hereditary. This means that if your child suffers from celiac disease, there is a very high likelihood that you, your partner, or someone else in your family has the same condition, but this isn't the only cause. Also, celiac disease isn't something that emerges at a specific age—rather, a person can develop celiac disease at any age. If you remember, I developed this condition in my thirties. Sometimes, though, it can emerge in children, and if you're reading this book, it likely means that your child has already been diagnosed with celiac disease.

Studies are being conducted to understand the role genetics plays in the occurrence of celiac disease. While previous research has helped us better understand this condition, we are still **searching for more answers** to enlighten us in terms of how to develop a gene mapping strategy for this disease. Apart from genetics, the environment can play an important role in triggering celiac disease. In such a case, gluten only happens to be a secondary factor in its development. In other words, although gluten does trigger celiac disease, the following environmental factors may have played a role in how the body developed an intolerance to gluten:

- Pregnancy and childbirth
- Severe stress
- Surgery
- Physical injury
- Infection

For children and adults who are at risk for this disease, celiac disease screening should be included as part of their routine physical exams. If you are still unsure if your child suffers from celiac disease, it's best to consult with their doctor. The sooner you confirm that your child has this condition, the sooner you can take the necessary steps to help them manage the condition. For instance, **if you can start your child on a gluten-free diet early on**, this can help prevent the potential damage gluten consumption will wreak on their small intestines. This is the most important benefit of making dietary changes as early as possible.

DID YOU KNOW? INTERESTING FACTS ABOUT CELIAC DISEASE

The more you learn about celiac disease, the greater your understanding of it will be. This is important when you are trying to help yourself and your child manage the disease more effectively. When I researched celiac disease, I discovered so many interesting things. Although managing this condition isn't easy, educating myself helped me view it with a new perspective. Since you're also interested in learning about celiac disease, here are **some key facts** for you to discover:

Celiac disease is very common in people from Europe

This is one of the more interesting facts I learned about celiac disease. According to recent studies, this disease is more prominent in Europe, especially in people of Northern European descent. The condition is also quite common in Asian, Hispanic, and African-American populations. Celiac disease occurring more commonly in specific populations makes a lot of sense, especially since the condition is hereditary.

People who suffer from celiac disease don't have a gluten allergy

One of the most common misconceptions about celiac disease is that people who suffer from it are simply allergic to gluten. This just isn't true. Celiac disease is an autoimmune disease wherein the body starts producing antibodies that attack itself when the person consumes gluten. Of course, there is such a thing as a gluten allergy, which is also quite severe.

Celiac disease isn't something your child will "grow out of"

Sadly, if you discover that your child suffers from celiac disease, you should learn to accept it—and help your child accept it, too. This will make it easier for you to guide your child as they transition to a gluten-free diet. As of now, following this diet is the most effective way to manage celiac disease and prevent its harmful effects on the body.

The symptoms of celiac disease are extremely varied

Surprisingly, celiac disease has more than 200 different signs and symptoms! Some sufferers experience several symptoms, some experience only a few, and others even have symptoms that are non-gastrointestinal. And a lucky few don't even experience any symptoms at all. However, for such people, this isn't a good thing in the long run. If a person doesn't know that they have celiac disease, they won't know that the gluten they are consuming is already causing slow and steady damage to their body. When you look at it this way, it might be better to experience the symptoms because you will be compelled to consult with a doctor to find out what's wrong.

Celiac disease is the only type of autoimmune disease for which experts have identified the genetic and environmental triggers

When it comes to autoimmune diseases, celiac disease stands out as it is the one that is most researched all over the world. It also happens to be the only disease of its kind in which researchers have identified gluten as the main environmental trigger. Also, researchers have come to the conclusion that this disease has a hereditary aspect, as this condition tends to run in the family.

Those who smoke cigarettes have a lower risk of developing celiac disease

Although researchers have yet to find out the reason, smokers are less likely to develop celiac disease compared to those who don't smoke. However, this doesn't mean that smoking will cure celiac disease. Remember that smoking isn't a healthy habit and even if it might help you avoid celiac disease, it will have other adverse effects on your body and your overall health.

The only treatment for celiac disease is a gluten-free diet

Since celiac disease is a chronic condition, there is nothing you or your child's doctor can do to cure it. The best thing you can do to help your child manage this condition is to help them transition into a gluten-free diet and adhere to this diet permanently. However, there are people who don't respond to this diet. In such cases, they have to consult with their doctor to come up with a plan for how to manage their disease more effectively. As your child follows the gluten-free diet, you must observe them to see if they are responding well. Otherwise, you may have to find other ways to help your child.

Gluten tends to cause damage to our bodies, whether we suffer from celiac disease or not

According to researchers, the consumption of gluten may cause intestinal permeability, whether you suffer from celiac disease or not. However, for those who don't suffer from this condition, their bodies can overcome or even heal from this damage. But for those with gluten sensitivity or celiac disease, the damage doesn't go away.

Instead, it keeps getting worse the more they consume gluten.

Left unchecked or untreated, celiac disease may lead to severe effects

When it comes to celiac disease, early diagnosis is important. If this condition is diagnosed early—like if your child's doctor discovers that they have celiac disease early on—you can already take the necessary steps to manage it. For those who don't find out, this condition may lead to other severe effects or conditions like thyroid disease, type 1 diabetes, anemia, multiple sclerosis, infertility, epilepsy, and even cancer. Since celiac disease may develop at any age, this can pose a challenge to those who are at risk for this condition.

Those who suffer from celiac disease don't have to avoid gluten completely

As you help your child transition to a gluten-free diet, you will have to be more careful with the foods you feed them. For instance, if you see something labeled, "gluten-free," this means that it only contains less than 20 parts per million of gluten. This amount is considered the "safe" threshold for those who suffer from celiac disease. Of course, if you can eliminate gluten altogether, that would be ideal.

As you can see, there is more to celiac disease than most people know. But the condition doesn't have to be a mystery to you—by discovering these things, you learn that it is something you can manage, because you know all about it!

DEALING WITH CELIAC DISEASE

If you or any member of your family suffers from celiac disease, it's important to talk about this with your child's doctor. That way, the doctor can include the required screening to diagnose celiac disease as early as possible. Remember, early detection is key.

Aside from knowing that your child is at risk, you should also keep a close eye on how your child reacts to foods that contain gluten. If you see that your child experiences adverse side effects after eating food that contains gluten, they might be suffering from this chronic condition. As a parent, it's important for you to be aware of these two factors so that you can ensure your child's health and safety.

As you already know, the only way to treat or manage celiac disease effectively is by following a gluten-free diet. Even if your child was eating gluten before you found out about their condition, transitioning to this diet can help your child's small intestine heal while preventing inflammation and other issues in the future. While on a gluten-free diet, your child will have to avoid foods that contain wheat, along with the following other grains:

- Barley
- Malt
- Durum
- Rye
- Farina
- Semolina
- Graham flour

Before you start transitioning your child to this specialized diet, you should first consult with their doctor. Even if you have already known for some time that your child has celiac disease, it's still helpful to talk to a medical professional. After reading this book, you can have a more informed conversation and even come up with a plan for how to help your child transition smoothly.

Even for adults, transitioning to a gluten-free diet can be challenging, especially if this diet is far from what they are used to. The good news is since you are reading this book right now, it means that you are **already slowly learning** everything you can about the disease. This is the all-important first step you need to take. Since it would be overwhelming to educate your child about all the ins and outs of celiac disease, you should do the learning for them.

Then, as you guide them into the gluten-free diet, you can start sharing everything you have learned about **the disease with them**, little by little.

After doing research, start coming up with a plan to help your child make the transition. If you have already been eating gluten-free foods once in a while, things become easier. But if this is your first time **encountering** a gluten-free diet, then you have to learn more about what foods to eat and what to avoid. The best thing for you to do is to learn how to make gluten-free meals and snacks for your child. That way, you can always be sure that nothing your child is eating contains any gluten.

At some point, though, you may want to give your child packaged gluten-free foods. This is okay, too, especially if you're too busy to prepare homemade meals or if your child is requesting such food products. When buying gluten-free snacks, you should learn how to read labels. This allows you to find any hidden ingredients that contain gluten to ensure that you are always feeding your child the right types of food. If you feel like you need help with planning your child's meals, you can consult their doctor or with a registered dietitian.

If you want your child to stick with the gluten-free diet, you may want to follow it with them. If you can encourage your whole family to follow the same diet, that would be even better. Over time, your child will get used to the diet and will feel more comfortable following it. When this happens, things will become easier for you, too. Living with celiac disease doesn't have to be a challenge. You can think of it as a way to make sure that your child doesn't have to deal with health problems in the future—because you are doing what is necessary now to teach them healthy food habits.

Part of helping your child transition to a gluten-free diet is to educate them about their condition. Every time your child has questions about celiac disease (and they will ask questions), you should have answers for them. Each time you plan to introduce something new to their diet, explain its importance. With each step you take, letting your child know why you're taking that step will make them more open and willing to take those steps with you. Soon, you will realize that your child is already doing well on the gluten-free diet and all you have to do is keep encouraging them to move forward.

UNDERSTANDING OTHER AUTO-IMMUNE DISORDERS

Each day, more and more people discover that they are suffering from some type of autoimmune disorder, not just celiac disease. But there are also cases where other types of autoimmune disease pair themselves with celiac disease.

Usually, this happens in people who don't know that they suffer from celiac disease and they don't seek treatment for it. In any case, since celiac disease isn't the only risk you (or your child) face, it's important to learn about the **many different kinds of autoimmune diseases existing** too. These include:

Addison's Disease

This disease primarily targets the adrenal glands, which are responsible for the production of aldosterone, cortisol, and androgen hormones. When the body doesn't have enough aldosterone, this may lead to excess potassium and sodium loss. When the body doesn't have enough cortisol, it isn't able to use and store glucose and carbohydrates properly. When either of these things happens, a person may experience symptoms like unexplained weight loss, low levels of blood sugar, weakness, and fatigue.

Autoimmune Vasculitis

This disease primarily targets the blood vessels. It is characterized by inflammation that narrows the veins and arteries, which restricts the flow of blood throughout the body.

Inflammatory Bowel Disease

This describes a number of conditions that cause the lining of the intestinal wall to become inflamed. There are different types of inflammatory bowel disease which affect different parts of the gastrointestinal tract.

Graves' Disease

This disease primarily targets the thyroid gland, causing an overproduction of thyroid hormones. When this happens, it revs up the body's functions and activities, causing the person to have symptoms like rapid weight loss, a rapid heartbeat, nervousness, and an intolerance to heat.

Hashimoto's Thyroiditis

This disease also targets the thyroid gland, but this time, it causes a reduction in the production of hormones. Because of this, the common symptoms a person may experience are goiter (thyroid swelling), hair loss, weight gain, fatigue, and a sensitivity to cold.

Multiple Sclerosis

This disease comes in a number of forms. Generally, it occurs when the myelin sheath in a person's central nervous system gets damaged. When this happens, the speed of transmission of messages between the brain, body, and spinal cord slows down. People who suffer from this condition may experience symptoms like balance issues, weakness, and numbness, for example.

Myasthenia Gravis

This disease primarily targets the nerve impulses in charge of helping with muscle control. People with this autoimmune disease will experience muscle weakness, especially when performing physical activity. With rest, such symptoms may improve.

Pernicious Anemia

This disease is characterized by a protein deficiency, specifically a type of protein that is produced by the cells in the stomach lining which helps with the absorption of vitamin B12. Without adequate amounts of vitamin B12, the person's body will experience an alteration in their ability to properly synthesize DNA. This condition is more common in people over 60 years old.

Psoriasis or Psoriatic Arthritis

This disease occurs when there is an overproduction of skin cells. When this happens, the extra cells accumulate and form into scales of plaque or inflamed patches on the skin. Other symptoms of this condition include pain in the joints, stiffness, and swelling.

Rheumatoid Arthritis

This disease primarily targets the joints, causing symptoms like stiffness, warmth, redness, and soreness. The condition can develop in people as young as 30, sometimes even younger than that.

Sjögren's Syndrome

This disease targets the glands responsible for lubricating the mouth and eyes. Therefore, it may cause dry mouth or dry eyes. In some cases, it also affects a person's skin or joints.

Systemic Lupus Erythematosus

This disease is quite severe as it affects various parts of the body like the heart, brain, joints, and kidneys. Apart from rashes, the most common symptoms of this disease are fatigue and joint pain.

Type 1 Diabetes

This disease targets the cells that produce insulin, which causes the body to lose its ability to regulate its levels of blood sugar. When a person's blood sugar levels remain elevated, it causes damage to the kidneys, eyes, heart, nerves, and blood vessels.

As you can see, there are so many autoimmune diseases that exist—and these are only the most common ones! As much as possible, you want to avoid these diseases, especially from occurring alongside celiac disease. This is why it's crucial to have yourself and your child checked. This is especially true if you experience some of the most common symptoms of autoimmune diseases, such as skin changes, fatigue, unexplained weight loss or weight gain, joint or muscle pain, and digestive discomfort or pain.

Remember, getting an early diagnosis allows you to take the necessary steps to treat or manage the condition. That way, it doesn't become more severe as time goes by.

ENTER, GLUTEN

Gluten refers to a group of proteins that can be found in rye, barley, wheat, and other types of grains. Gluten gives pasta, pastries, and bread their chewiness and elasticity, making them more appealing to eat. Although most people don't have any noticeable issues with gluten, there are some who should avoid it because of how gluten affects their bodies. Apart from those who suffer from celiac disease, people who suffer from non-celiac gluten sensitivity and wheat allergy should also avoid foods that contain gluten. If your child suffers from celiac disease or their doctor has recommended a gluten-free diet for them, watch out for these foods that contain gluten:

Barley

You can find this in beer, brewer's yeast, food coloring, malt, and soups.

Rye

You can find this in cereals, rye beer, and rye bread.

Triticale

You can find this in bread, cereals, and pasta.

Wheat

You can find this in baked goods, bread, cereals, pasta, roux, salad dressings, sauces, and soups.

Sometimes, gluten can find its way in oats, especially those grown with barley, rye, triticale, and wheat. Because of this, you should always look for gluten-free oats when you need this ingredient for your recipes.

If you discover that your child has celiac disease, you might start seeing gluten as "the enemy." But when you think about it, how did gluten become such a huge part of our lives?

The truth is, although gluten can be found in so many of the foods that we consume today, it hasn't been part of our diets for very long. Our ancient ancestors only ate foods that they hunted, gathered or foraged. Back then, they hadn't learned how to process grains yet, which means that gluten wasn't part of their diets. This particular group of proteins was only introduced into our diet around 10,000 years ago, when we learned how to process grains for consumption. When you think about it, this probably means that celiac disease and other gluten-related diseases **only emerged at roughly the same time**. Before gluten was introduced into our diets, people didn't have to worry about the **adverse side effects** of consuming gluten because they weren't eating it in the first place! But now that it is part of our lives, **all we can do is learn how to deal with it**.

WHEN CELIAC DISEASE AND GLUTEN MEET

For people who suffer from celiac disease, certain proteins are toxic to them. Collectively, these proteins are known as prolamins, and the grains that contain these toxic proteins have their own unique fractions of prolamins. Barley contains hordein, rye contains secalin, and wheat contains gliadin. If a celiac disease sufferer ingests these grains, the gluten content starts doing damage to their body.

Normally, the body can digest proteins with the help of digestive enzymes. These enzymes break proteins down into amino acids known as peptides. These peptides are then broken down further so that the body can absorb and transport them as needed. However, prolamins contain glutamine and proline—two types of amino acids that are hard to digest. What's more, neither glutamine and proline are considered essential amino acids. Foods that contain gluten are rich in these prolamins, which makes them more difficult to digest. In fact, the digestive enzymes of the body aren't even able to break these proteins down completely. While this isn't an obvious problem for most people, it causes adverse side effects to those suffering from celiac disease.

Generally, everyone reacts to gluten in different ways. For most people, it's just something that the body cannot digest completely. But for others, their bodies perceive gluten as a toxin, and this is when their immune system starts attacking itself. If a person continues consuming gluten because they don't know that they are suffering from celiac disease, their immune system will just keep on attacking itself until inflammation and **damage emerges**. This is when the person will start experiencing the common symptoms of celiac disease, which include bloating, bowel movement issues, fatigue, intestinal damage, unexplained weight loss, and malnutrition. Then, there are those who don't suffer from celiac disease but still experience adverse side effects from gluten consumption. These people may suffer from the following conditions:

Dermatitis herpetiformis

People who suffer from this condition get an itchy skin rash after consuming gluten. If it persists (probably because the person continues to consume gluten), the rash may start producing bumps and blisters.

Non-celiac gluten sensitivity

This is also known as gluten intolerance or gluten-sensitive enteropathy. A person who suffers from this condition may experience similar symptoms to those who suffer from celiac disease, except for intestinal damage.

Wheat allergy

People who suffer from wheat allergy won't just experience adverse effects from consuming gluten. Generally, they are allergic to other types of proteins, too, such as globulin, albumin, and gliadin, all of which are found in wheat. The symptoms of this condition vary greatly, but some of the most common ones are hives, itching or swelling of the throat or mouth, breathing difficulties, itchy eyes, diarrhea, anaphylaxis, nausea, and cramps.

Basically, if you or your child suffers from celiac disease or any of the conditions mentioned above, staying away from gluten is your best and smartest option. While this may take a lot of adjustments and effort from you, what you get in return is worth it. If you want to ensure your long-term health and well-being, avoiding gluten is key.

THE WONDERS OF GOING GLUTEN-FREE

Right now, the gluten-free diet is trending all over the world, and for good reason. Going gluten-free isn't just hype, as this diet offers a number of great health benefits even to those who don't suffer from celiac disease. This means you can make it easier for your child to transition to a gluten-free diet by following the diet along with them.

As I mentioned at the beginning of this book, when I experienced the benefits of the gluten-free diet, I wished I had started following it earlier. Although gluten has been introduced in our diets for some time now, more people are becoming aware of the marketing ploys of food **companies that produce food containing gluten**. With this awareness, these people are also starting to question the true effect of gluten on the body. They have also started wondering about the long-term health impacts of gluten even though they don't suffer from celiac disease or any kind of condition that causes them to feel adverse side effects.

The good news is, going gluten-free isn't as challenging as it was in the past. A few years ago, gluten-free foods could only be found in health stores and specialty food shops. But now, you can find these food items virtually everywhere. Even in restaurants, you can find gluten-free options, making it easier for you and your child to start your gluten-free journey. You can even tell your child that it's 'hip' to go gluten-free, as more people are doing it. Hopefully, this will make your child feel more positive about the dietary change you are about to help them transition into.

By going gluten-free, you will do more than just give up pizza, pasta, cereals, beer, and other obvious foods that contain gluten. To help your child avoid gluten and enjoy all the benefits of a gluten-free diet, you have to be very careful with what you buy, especially when it comes to store-bought foods. Unfortunately, gluten can also be found in other food products like soy sauce, frozen veggies in sauces, supplements, and foods that contain "natural flavorings." These are the things that make following a gluten-free diet more challenging than it should be.

By reading this book, you have already started learning how to help your child follow a gluten-free diet. Everything you learn about the diet will guide you, but it can also lead to challenges, especially if you only look at the good side of going gluten-free. When you read most resources, you will get the idea that going gluten-free almost seems like a no-brainer. There is some truth to this, but you can prepare yourself even more by knowing both sides of the story. Going gluten-free is a wonderful thing, especially if your child suffers from celiac disease—but you need to be well-informed before you take the necessary steps to make this change.

THE PROS AND CONS OF A GLUTEN-FREE DIET

If you are planning to start following a diet, or you're planning to start your child on a diet, you should make it a point to learn everything you can about it. Understanding only the benefits of these diets will catch you off-guard, especially if you start experiencing challenges you didn't even know about. By learning the good and bad, you will arm yourself with the knowledge you need to make a realistic plan to help your child. Also, if you are already aware of both the benefits and downsides of the diet you're interested in—a gluten-free diet, in this case—you will have realistic expectations as you start the journey. In this chapter, you will learn more about the gluten-free diet from different perspectives.

THE GLUTEN-FREE CRAZE

These days, the gluten-free diet is all the rage. Although it is recommended for people who have issues with gluten, even those who don't have started following the diet. From celebrities to health enthusiasts and "regular people," this diet is being touted by individuals from all walks of life. Apart from being the essential diet choice for those with celiac disease, wheat allergy, and non-celiac gluten sensitivity, some evidence suggests that this diet may also help those who suffer from various gastrointestinal problems.

Then, there are those who have decided to go gluten-free because it's trendy and they think it will help them achieve their weight-loss goals. However, this isn't one of the main benefits of the gluten-free diet. After all, gluten-free doesn't necessarily mean low sodium, low sugar or low fat. As a matter of fact, a lot of gluten-free products typically contain more sugar and fat to give them the same texture and taste as foods that contain gluten. So if you're thinking about going gluten-free because you want to lose weight, you may want to consider other options.

Before making the choice to follow this diet, you should first know your reason for doing so. For instance, if your child's doctor recommended this diet because they suffer from celiac disease, this is the best possible reason. Otherwise, there are things you should consider before embarking on this unique diet craze. Here are some points for you to keep in mind as you think about this diet choice:

The science behind gluten intolerance or sensitivity isn't conclusive

Those who suffer from celiac disease shouldn't consume gluten, whether or not they experience symptoms of the condition. If they continue consuming this group of proteins, their immune systems will continue attacking until they develop irreparable damage in their small intestines.

But for those who suffer from "gluten intolerance" or "gluten sensitivity," the science behind the choice to switch to a diet that is completely free of gluten isn't as conclusive. Although these people can choose to follow the diet, it may not be necessary. These people may still consume gluten in small amounts so as not to trigger their symptoms. Otherwise, they don't have to make such a huge change to their current diets. Of course, if you just want to be sure or you don't want to risk it, the choice is entirely up to you. Just prepare yourself for all the challenges and adjustments that come with the diet.

This diet won't help you achieve your weight-loss goals

Although I have mentioned this already, it's worth emphasizing, especially since weight loss is the most common reason why people choose to start new diets. Again, if this is your main reason, you should consider other diets that can help you shed those stubborn excess pounds.

The gluten-free diet comes with a number of potential health risks

Those who suffer from celiac disease follow a gluten-free diet with the recommendation and guidance of their doctors. If you plan to follow this diet "just because," then you should educate yourself to ensure that you follow it properly. Otherwise, instead of enjoying the potential health benefits of this diet, you might experience the potential health risks such as nutrient deficiencies, constipation, and you might even compromise your immune system function.

Despite the fad, gluten is still found in many food items

Popular as the gluten-free diet is right now, a lot of people don't really know what it truly entails. For most people (especially those who don't need to follow the diet), they simply opt for foods that are labeled gluten-free then say that they are following a special new diet. However, even these food products may contain gluten. If you were serious about going gluten-free, you should learn how to read food labels and ask the right questions to ensure that you are truly consuming food that is free of gluten.

After considering all of these things, if you still want to go gluten-free, then it's time to start learning and planning. The same thing goes if you want your child to follow the gluten-free diet because their doctor has recommended it.

IS YOUR CHILD GLUTEN-INTOLERANT?

Gluten intolerance can vary in severity and you can see this in the types of symptoms that will manifest. If your child suffers from gluten intolerance, you may notice that they are complaining about the same things over and over again. Celiac disease is a form of gluten intolerance, and it also happens to be the most severe. If your child has already been diagnosed with celiac disease, then you should already know what to do. But if you aren't sure yet, here are the symptoms to look out for:

Abdominal pain

This is one of the most common symptoms of gluten intolerance, but it can also indicate a number of other conditions. To determine if your child's abdominal pain is connected to gluten intolerance, try to observe your child after they consume gluten. If they complain of abdominal pain after a meal or snack that contains gluten, then gluten intolerance is a definite possibility.

Bowel issues

These include constipation, diarrhea, and even smelly feces. Although experiencing these symptoms occasionally is normal, if they keep happening to your child, this may indicate gluten intolerance. Remember, gluten causes inflammation and damage to the small intestine—and this may cause a number of bowel issues.

Bloating

If your child always complains that they feel like they're full of gas or their tummy is swollen, this will make them feel extremely uncomfortable. This is another common symptom of various diseases including celiac disease and other forms of gluten intolerance.

Feeling Tired or Fatigued

Children are normally full of energy throughout the day. But if you notice that your child always seems tired, there might be an underlying cause. This is especially true if their tiredness or fatigue comes after consuming gluten.

Skin changes

Sometimes, celiac disease can manifest in the form of dermatitis herpetiformis, a type of skin blistering condition. But this isn't the only skin change or condition that can indicate gluten intolerance. Other conditions are psoriasis, alopecia areata, and chronic urticaria.

Frequent headaches

Children seldom get headaches or migraines unless they are suffering from another condition such as gluten intolerance. If your child is always telling you that they have a headache, pay attention. Consult with your child's doctor right away to find out the cause of this symptom.

Unexplained weight loss

By far, this is one of the most troubling symptoms, especially with children. Again, unexplained weight loss can be caused by a number of factors. Since celiac disease can lead to poor nutrient absorption, you may notice your child losing weight even though they are eating normally.

Brain fog

Brain fog occurs when a person isn't able to think clearly. In children, they might have trouble focusing, understanding you, or remembering things. This is another troubling symptom, especially for children since this is the time when they need to be observant and learn new things as they are growing up.

These aren't the only symptoms of gluten intolerance and celiac disease. Remember that this condition has hundreds of symptoms, which means that as a parent, you have to be very observant of your child. Other symptoms that might manifest include:

- Agitation and frequent mood swings
- Anxiety or depression
- Autoimmune disorders
- Delayed puberty or unexplained short stature
- Iron-deficiency anemia
- Numbness of the legs or arms
- Pain in the muscles or joints

If your child complains of these symptoms or you have observed these symptoms in your child, you should consult with their doctor right away to get a proper diagnosis. Remember, when it comes to celiac disease, early detection is key.

GOING GLUTEN-FREE: A CHOICE OR A REQUIREMENT?

There is a big difference between choosing to follow the gluten-free diet or following it as a necessity. A person who suffers from celiac disease needs to follow this diet as a necessity. But other people, even those who suffer from other gluten-related conditions, can choose to follow the diet. For instance, if a person suffers from a wheat allergy, they may experience symptoms when their bodies react to a specific protein found in wheat. But this protein isn't always gluten.

Although a wheat allergy can cause severe symptoms, like breathing difficulties or even anaphylaxis, a person who has this condition doesn't necessarily have to follow a gluten-free diet. Instead, they should find out what is really causing their allergic reactions. If the person is merely intolerant of wheat, they may only experience mild symptoms and discomfort. If you think your child only has a wheat allergy, you should still consult with their doctor to find out what you need to do to help your child manage their condition.

The same thing goes if you think your child is suffering from gluten intolerance or non-celiac gluten sensitivity. You should still consult with your child's doctor. When you visit your child's doctor, you have to give them your child's whole history, especially the symptoms they have experienced. This will give the doctor a better idea of what your child's condition could be and what tests to perform. If your child is diagnosed with celiac disease, then you can start helping them transition into a gluten-free diet. Since celiac disease isn't something that can be cured or something that your child will grow out of, you have to help them learn how to live with this condition.

Getting such news doesn't have to make you or your child stressed. As a parent, you have to help your child understand their disease and learn the importance of managing it through their diet. If you can help them eliminate gluten by following this essential diet, your child doesn't have to experience the painful and harmful symptoms. Yes, it will be a long and challenging journey. But, with your help, your child can get through this and grow up to be a well-adjusted adult who follows a healthy, balanced, gluten-free diet.

HEALTH BENEFITS OF THE GLUTEN-FREE DIET

If your child's doctor has diagnosed them with celiac disease, it's important to take the necessary steps to eliminate it from their diet as soon as possible. Otherwise, they might experience a number of severe effects. Let's have a quick recap of these before moving on to how the gluten-free diet will make your child's life better:

- Inflammation of the gut
- Damage to their gut biome
- Long-term damage to their small intestine
- Painful or uncomfortable gut symptoms
- Other autoimmune reactions, like those affecting their skin or even their brains
- Increased risk of developing other types of autoimmune diseases

Many studies have been conducted around celiac disease and the gluten-free diet. Most of these studies have concluded that this diet is highly beneficial for people who suffer from celiac disease. One particular study involved healthy participants who were asked to follow the gluten-free diet for four weeks (Bonder, M. J., et. al., 2016). Just like the other studies, this one showed that the gluten-free diet can provide good changes in the body. But for sufferers of celiac disease, you already know that the gluten-free diet is a requirement. You already know why this is so, now let's go through the benefits of the gluten-free diet, especially for those who need to follow it:

To promote healthy weight gain

One of the common symptoms of celiac disease is unexplained weight loss, and this happens due to poor nutrient absorption. Naturally, if you eliminate gluten from your child's diet, their body will heal, their immune system will stop initiating attacks, and adequate nutrient absorption will resume. When this happens, your child will start regaining the weight they have lost. Once your child reaches a healthy weight, you can maintain this through a healthy, balanced diet that's free of gluten.

To improve energy levels

If your child suffers from celiac disease, you may also notice that they are always weak, tired, or fatigued. Again, these symptoms are caused by the internal reactions and damage happening inside your child's body. As you eliminate gluten from their diet, you will notice that your child's energy levels are increasing. Once again, they will have the energy to get through each day along with a newfound enthusiasm for life.

To eliminate bloating

Bloating is extremely uncomfortable and sometimes, it can even be painful. Another benefit of the gluten-free diet is that it helps eliminate bloating. Since your child won't be consuming gluten anymore, they won't experience reactions like digestive distress. This, in turn, means that they will no longer experience swelling, pain, or discomfort caused by bloating.

To reduce the risk of developing lactose intolerance

Often, those who suffer from celiac disease also develop lactose intolerance. The reason for this is that the lining of the stomach produces lactase, the enzyme responsible for breaking down lactose in milk, cheese, and other dairy products. Since gluten damages this lining, their bodies cannot produce this important enzyme. Therefore, they develop an intolerance. Fortunately, the gluten-free diet can help your child heal so that they don't have to develop this condition that will prevent them from enjoying dairy products.

To improve the health of their bones

If a child suffers from celiac disease without knowing it, they may develop severe nutrient deficiencies—and a calcium deficiency will compromise the health of their bones. For children, this is very dangerous as it will cause delays in their growth and development. In adults, it may lead to issues like osteopenia or osteoporosis. By following a gluten-free diet, your child can maintain a healthy bone mineral density.

To improve the health of their skin

As you now know, celiac disease can also cause changes in your child's skin, usually for the worse. But with the right diet, you may notice an amelioration in your child's skin health—you may even see their skin conditions fading away on their own.

To prevent hair loss

Hair loss is another potential side effect of celiac disease and just like most other symptoms, this is due to nutritional deficiencies. Apart from preventing hair loss, the gluten-free diet can also improve your child's hair texture while increasing their hair density.

To reduce the frequency of headaches

Headaches and migraines will surely have an adverse effect on your child. Generally, children don't experience these symptoms unless they are suffering from an undiagnosed condition. These symptoms stem from the gut-brain connection that exists within the body. Since your child's gut is suffering because of the disease, it will eventually take a toll on their brain, as well. Fortunately, the gluten-free diet will also help reduce the frequency of these headaches or even eliminate them completely.

To prevent joint pain

Although children might be too young to suffer from joint pain, this is still a possibility. As a parent, you want to avoid this at all costs because joint pain isn't something any child should have to deal with. By guiding your child into a gluten-free diet, you are also helping them avoid this symptom. Even as an adult, you can take advantage of this benefit as you will feel your joint pain fading away the longer you stick with the diet.

To prevent anxiety and depression

If a child experiences all of the symptoms and side effects of celiac disease, they may also start developing anxiety or depression. Again, you want to prevent these conditions as they are very difficult to overcome. You can do this by encouraging your child to stick with the gluten-free diet so that none of the symptoms will manifest.

Other benefits

When it comes to the gluten-free diet, the benefits just keep coming, especially for those with celiac disease. Aside from the ones we have already discussed, other potential benefits include:

- More focus on whole foods like fruits and veggies, which are naturally gluten-free

- Elimination of processed and unhealthy foods from your child's diet
- Overall improvement of digestive health
- Healthy cholesterol levels
- Reduced risk of diabetes, heart disease, and certain cancers
- Improved awareness of healthy food choices through the diet

It is significantly noticeable how the gluten-free diet has grown in popularity. In the past, people didn't pay much attention to gluten. But now, you can find gluten-free foods, recipes, and information everywhere you look. With all of these benefits to look forward to, encouraging your child to go gluten-free makes sense, right? But before you start, let's take a look at the other side of the coin.

THE POTENTIAL DOWNSIDES YOU SHOULD KNOW ABOUT

In recent years, the gluten-free diet has become a huge trend. It evolved from something that people didn't even consider into something they want to follow for their own personal reasons. Now that you have reached this far, you already understand that this diet isn't like the other trendy diets all over the world—the gluten-free diet is considered a necessity for a select group of people.

Those who don't understand the gluten-free diet completely may start following it with their own goals in mind, such as weight loss. Of course, now you know that this diet isn't the best choice for this particular goal. While the gluten-free diet can improve various aspects of your health, there are a few major risks you must know about before making your final choice. These are:

Nutritional deficiencies

The gluten-free diet can easily turn into an unbalanced diet because it involves eliminating all foods that contain gluten. If you don't plan this diet well, you will end up developing various nutrient deficiencies. For instance, if you simply eliminate all foods that contain gluten and replace these with processed foods that are labeled "gluten-free" without checking their nutrient content, you will surely miss out on essential nutrients. Over time, instead of experiencing improvements in your health, you might experience the exact opposite. Sadly, most people who end up developing nutrient deficiencies blame the diet without acknowledging the fact that they didn't educate themselves to ensure they followed the diet correctly.

Gluten withdrawal

Since gluten has become a part of our lives since it first came to be, we have all gotten used to it. Now, if you suddenly eliminate gluten from your diet, you may experience symptoms of withdrawal. Extreme as it might seem, this is what some people do. They make a choice to go gluten-free on a whim and they stop eating all foods that contain gluten. Although the gluten-free diet can potentially improve your health, doing something this drastic causes withdrawal, which comes with its own challenging symptoms and side effects.

Toxicity

This risk comes from the increase of potentially toxic or deleterious compounds due to the reduction of your food options. For one, if you increase your consumption of rice and fish, you may also be increasing your consumption of heavy metals like mercury, arsenic, cadmium, and lead. Another significant source of potentially toxic compounds is processed gluten-free foods. These usually contain additives that, when ingested in high amounts, can have toxic effects on your body. Although more research is needed to prove this particular risk of the gluten-free diet, it's still something you should look out for if you decide to go gluten-free.

Risk to your mental health

Since the gluten-free diet isn't the easiest diet to follow, it might pose a risk to your mental health. As you force yourself to adhere to this diet without having a strong reason to do so, you could put yourself at risk mentally. Although you might be making some improvements to your physical health, would you be willing to compromise your mental health in the process? If not (and you shouldn't), you should consider following an easier diet—one that will help you achieve your health goals. With such a diet, you will feel more motivated and even happier once you see that all of your efforts are moving you closer to your goals.

Making the choice to follow a gluten-free diet just because it's trendy isn't a valid reason. More importantly, making a choice to start your child on this diet even though their doctor hasn't recommended it is definitely a no-no, too. Think about this decision, as it is something that will change your life in the long run. Since it also involves a lot of adjustments, you have to commit to this diet once you have decided to follow it.

The bottom line is this: you should have the right reasons for following the gluten-free diet. If you have these reasons, then you should create a plan for how to follow—or help your child follow—the diet correctly.

OTHER TREATMENTS FOR CELIAC DISEASE

As you know, you can only confirm that your child suffers from celiac disease through a proper diagnosis from your child's doctor. Once the doctor makes this diagnosis, the next thing they will do is to recommend that your child be placed on a gluten-free diet. As a parent, the mere thought of putting your child on a specialized diet can feel overwhelming. This is normal. All parents have felt this way. And when you think about all of the foods that you will have to eliminate from your child's diet, things can get even more overwhelming.

But, if you want your child to learn how to manage their condition while avoiding complications, you must help them follow and stick with this diet. With your guidance and support, you will be able to help your child with their condition. Still, even with everything you learn in this book, you will need to communicate with your child's doctor and even a dietitian to come up with a plan for your child's gluten-free journey.

The most effective and only treatment for celiac disease is a gluten-free diet. In other words, to prevent celiac disease from getting worse (because there is no cure for it), you must eliminate all gluten from your child's diet. For a lot of people, following this diet causes their symptoms to disappear completely. Then, the damage caused by gluten starts to heal and they start feeling better, too. As a matter of fact, you will see improvements to your child's health in as little as a week after they start the diet. Also, if your child starts following this diet early, there is a higher likelihood that they will heal completely, unlike adults who have received their diagnosis later in life.

For those who suffer from celiac disease, the gluten-free diet will remain a permanent part of their lives. If they try to eat food that contains gluten, the symptoms they have overcome can easily return. This is why you need to keep encouraging your child to stick with the diet. But aside from this diet, there is one more thing you can do to help your child manage their condition better, or at least ensure that their health isn't compromised because of this diet. After your doctor informs you about your child's diagnosis, you can ask them about the possibility of giving your child supplements to prevent nutrient deficiencies. Since nutrient deficiency is the biggest risk of the gluten-free diet, you want to avoid this, too. For those who follow this diet, the most common supplements are:

- Calcium
- Fiber
- Folate
- Iron

- Magnesium
- Niacin
- Vitamin D
- Zinc

Ask your doctor if you have to pair your child's diet with any of these supplements or any other supplements that they can recommend. But if you can ensure that your child will get all the nutrients they need from the food they eat, supplementing with vitamins might not be necessary.

The beauty of the gluten-free diet is that children who suffer from celiac disease tend to respond to it very well. Although you won't see these results overnight, you will notice that your child is becoming healthier and happier because the uncomfortable and painful symptoms are beginning to fade. Also, your child's growth and development will soon normalize after their body has healed. This is definitely something to look forward to.

3

EMPOWERING YOUR CHILD TO CHOOSE HEALTH

By this point, you have already learned the fundamentals of celiac disease and the gluten-free diet. Now, it's time to start thinking about how you will guide and help your child with their transition. Right now, your goal is to introduce the diet to your child and explain why it's important for them to follow. But your long-term goal should be to empower your child so that they will always choose health. This ensures your child will continue to follow the diet even as they grow up. Since the gluten-free diet will be a lifelong aspect of your child to manage their celiac disease, accepting it and following it long-term is of the essence.

THE GLUTEN-FREE DIET FOR CHILDREN

Children should only start following a gluten-free diet if they suffer from celiac disease. If your child suffers from any other gluten-related condition, consult with your doctor first before you decide to change their diet. If your child is perfectly healthy, avoiding gluten won't give them more energy or make them "feel better." As a matter of fact, changing your child's diet unnecessarily might make things complicated for you, especially since you have to plan your child's diet more carefully. As you eliminate foods that contain gluten, you will have to find replacements for these foods to ensure that your child doesn't end up developing deficiencies.

Of course, if your child has celiac disease, it's a different story. You have to make the change, create a plan, and find healthy substitutes to keep your child's diet healthy and balanced. To do this, you should focus on getting your child used to eating whole foods instead of processed food products, even if they are labeled "gluten-free." For your child's snacks and meals, you should encourage them to eat fruits, veggies, lean protein, healthy fats, nuts, seeds, dairy products, and dishes that you have prepared in your own kitchen. Even at school, packing homemade meals for your child will make it easier for them to stick with the diet.

As you will soon discover, following the gluten-free diet can be a challenge, especially at the beginning. You will have to do a lot of convincing and encouraging to get your child to try new foods and wean them off foods they're used to that contain gluten. You will have to be patient, especially if your child doesn't understand how serious their condition is. At home, you will be your child's guide as they follow this specialized way of eating. But your work won't end at home.

If you want your child to be completely free of gluten, you should speak to your child's teacher, too. Inform your child's teacher about your child's condition and the doctor's recommendation to go gluten-free. If your child's teacher knows all about the gluten-free diet and celiac disease, good for you! If not, then you will have to help them out. Explain to your child's teacher what celiac disease is to help them understand the importance of your child's new diet. It's best to communicate openly with your child's teacher so that they can help you with this new endeavor. Be as helpful as possible by providing plans and resources to make things easier for your child's teacher, too. That way, they will be more willing to be part of this transition.

One thing you must remember when transitioning your child to a gluten-free diet is that this usually takes a lot of patience and observation. For most people, the transition may lead to a deterioration in their quality of life, especially if they aren't doing it willingly. As a parent, you must show your child that this change isn't a bad thing. It is meant to make them happier, healthier, and free of pain. As you guide your child, having a positive attitude will make them feel more positive, too. Then it will become easier for you to introduce new foods, eliminate unhealthy ones, and balance your child's diet to keep them healthy and strong.

HOW DOES THE GLUTEN-FREE DIET HELP CHILDREN?

For a lot of people, it seems like the gluten-free diet has suddenly exploded in popularity. In the past, people didn't pay much attention to gluten, but now, even those who don't have to avoid gluten have decided to join the gluten-free trend. Some parents even claim that the gluten-free diet helped change their children's behavior for the better! As you now know, if your child's doctor gives you the green light, you may choose to change your child's diet into one that doesn't include gluten. Children may experience the same benefits mentioned in the last chapter. But going gluten-free also has a number of additional unique benefits for them, including:

It will help tame your child's tummy

If a child who has celiac disease consumes gluten, this sets off a reaction that causes damage to their small intestine. Even if your child doesn't experience symptoms right away, the damage caused may eventually lead to discomfort, pain, bloating, and other more severe symptoms. Most children who suffer from celiac disease always complain of tummy aches and other similar issues. But when you start your child on the gluten-free diet, this can help tame their sensitive tummies. As time goes by, you will notice that your child seems healthier, more energized, and happier, too. This is one of the most significant benefits of going gluten-free.

It may be helpful for autistic children

Recently, the gluten-free diet has become quite popular in the autism community. There have been many anecdotal reports from parents that claim that following this diet helped improve the symptoms of their children. Most of these parents have also eliminated casein, a protein found in dairy products, from their children's diets.

Of course, these anecdotal reports need to have scientific evidence to back them up before we believe them completely. Right now, the reason behind the apparent effectiveness of the gluten-free diet to help children on the autism spectrum, there is a lack of information. If you are interested in this particular benefit for your child, consult with your child's doctor first. Ask them about the possibility of shifting your child to a gluten-free diet, as it might help with their symptoms. Before doing so, it would be best to research more on this benefit before your consultation so that you can have a more informed conversation.

It may be helpful for children with ADHD, too

Attention deficit hyperactivity disorder, or ADHD for short, is another very common condition that parents are constantly seeking help with. Some of these parents have tried putting their children on a gluten-free diet in hopes of helping with this disorder. If you remember, one of the common symptoms of celiac disease is brain fog, which causes children to seem inattentive, especially after consuming gluten. This is one possible reason why parents think that a gluten-free diet may help. However, experts agree that although the diet may help improve your child's overall feeling of well-being, it might not do anything to make them more attentive or reduce their hyperactivity. Again, it's best to consult your doctor before making any decisions.

With these benefits and the general benefits that both children and adults can look forward to, the gluten-free diet seems like an amazing dietary choice, don't you think? Just remember that these are *potential* benefits, and your child will only get to enjoy them if they follow the diet correctly. Since you will be taking away different types of food from your child's diet, you should also consider replacing these with nutrient-dense foods such as:

Dairy

Give your child dairy products like cheese, yogurt, and fortified milk, for example. These nutritious food items will help increase your child's nutrient consumption each day.

Fruits

Fruits are an essential part of your child's diet, whether they are frozen, canned, or dried. Of course, fresh fruits are still the best. Fruits are great because you can use them in various recipes. You can also slice fruits and serve them to your child for a simple, healthy snack. And since there are so many different types of fruits out there, your child will never get bored.

Gluten-free grains

While many grains don't belong in your child's diet, there are some exceptions. Whenever you use grains in recipes, make sure they are gluten-free. These days, it's easier to check because food labels already indicate if they are gluten-free or not. But if you really want to make sure, read the list of ingredients before buying any products that are supposedly gluten-free.

Healthy fats

Although most people avoid fat at all costs, this macronutrient is an essential part of our diet, especially for children. If you want to avoid excessive or unhealthy fats, focus on choosing healthy fat sources like avocados or fatty fish, for example.

Lean protein

When it comes to proteins, it's best to opt for lean options so you won't be adding unnecessary fats to your child's diet. Some examples are lean poultry, eggs, seafood, nuts, seeds, and soy products.

Vegetables

Just like fruits, you can serve your child frozen, canned, or dried veggies—but fresh veggies are still the best. There are so many different kinds of vegetables out there and they all contain an amazing array of nutrients. If your child isn't fond of veggies, find ways to make them feel more willing to eat their greens by adding them to delicious and interesting dishes.

Aside from choosing nutrient-dense foods, you should also try to limit your child's intake of added sugars, trans fats, and saturated fats. Usually, food items that contain these will only give your child empty calories. This can be very harmful, especially since your child is undergoing a diet transition. As much as possible, focus on whole, healthy foods.

Another way to make sure that your child will experience the benefits of the gluten-free diet is to observe and monitor them constantly, at least at the beginning of their gluten-free journey. Take note of any changes that are happening in your child, both good and bad. That way, when you have your regular checkup with your child's doctor, you can share how your child is adjusting to the diet.

THE RISE OF GLUTEN-FREE FOOD

As more people in the U.S. and the rest of the world are diagnosed with celiac disease, the gluten-free trend has matched this growth. Following a gluten-free diet might have been challenging in the past, but now, you'll be happy to know that gluten-free food is on the rise. Whether you go to supermarkets, farmers' markets, or health food stores, you will always find a section that offers gluten-free foods. Hopefully, this will make your child feel more comfortable about this new change they are making in their life.

The gluten-free diet is essential for children and adults who suffer from celiac disease. This is something you would have also learned if your child was diagnosed with this condition. If you are following a gluten-free diet even though you don't suffer from this disease, you may have your own reasons. For a lot of people, they follow it because going gluten-free has become a huge trend. In fact, even celebrities have joined this dietary trend! But if your reason for following the diet is to follow a trend, you shouldn't make the same decision for your child just so they can be trendy, too—unless your child's doctor agrees with you.

People who are perfectly healthy but want to follow a gluten-free diet need to be very careful. For instance, if you want to encourage your child to follow the diet by following it along with them, you will have to observe how your body reacts to this change. If your child needs to go gluten-free because they have celiac disease, you will most likely see improvements in their health. But you might not see the same positive effects as you follow the diet, too. As you plan your child's diet, you shouldn't neglect yours. Take this journey together to achieve your goal of better health for yourself and your child.

GO SHOPPING WITH YOUR CHILD

One of the most enjoyable and effective ways for you to encourage your child to follow the gluten-free diet is by taking them with you whenever you go grocery shopping.

This is a wonderful way to empower your child's knowledge of what is gluten-free, what isn't, and how varied your child's options are. Going shopping with your child will give you opportunities to explain what a gluten-free diet is all about and why it's important for your child to avoid foods that contain gluten. If you're not used to shopping for groceries with your child, this chore may take some getting used to. Here are some tips to help make your shopping experience easier and more enjoyable:

Visit all of the aisles with your child

This is a fun (although time-consuming) way to introduce your child to gluten-free foods. The first time you take your child shopping, make sure you set a schedule for it. Before you go to the grocery store, you should have already explained to your child that they have to start a new diet to help them feel better. That way, when you visit the different aisles in the grocery store, you can identify which foods are gluten-free and which aren't. You can even make a game out of it so that your child has fun while shopping.

In the grain section, choose high-fiber options that are gluten-free

The main sources of gluten are grains, but not all grains contain gluten. Grains are an essential part of your child's diet, especially if you want to avoid constipation. Fortunately, it's much easier to find gluten-free grains now—you just have to know what to look for. Some of the best high-fiber, gluten-free options are quinoa, millet, beans, amaranth, chickpeas, and whole-grain brown rice. You can use these as substitutes when following recipes.

Stay away from oats for now

Although oats are naturally gluten-free, they do contain avenin, a protein that has the same structure as gluten. At the beginning of your child's transition to a gluten-free diet, you may have to avoid oats. Once your child's symptoms have faded away, you can ask your child's doctor about reintroducing this food into their diet. Just make sure to buy gluten-free oats.

Learn how to read food labels

To ensure your child's safety, you should learn how to properly read food labels. This will go a long way toward eliminating gluten from your child's diet for good. This tip is very important since some food products that are labeled "gluten-free" aren't completely free of gluten. For instance, some flavorings used in sauces may contain wheat, which is one of the main sources of gluten. These are the things you must look out for as you read food labels while shopping. And as your child grows older, you can teach them this important skill, too.

Find ways to fill the gaps to avoid nutrient deficiencies

Replacements and substitutions are important while transitioning to a gluten-free diet. You don't want your child to end up developing a deficiency, so you must take a proactive approach. If you think your child won't get enough fiber, find a gluten-free fiber source. If you think your child needs more protein in their diet, find foods that are high in protein. It's all about finding the right balance to keep your child healthy.

In some cases, you might not be able to fill those gaps simply because you cannot force your child to eat everything you want them to eat. In such a case, you should (once again) consult with your child's doctor. They may recommend a multivitamin or refer you to a professional dietician or nutritionist. Then you can work together to come up with a healthy eating plan for your child to follow. Don't be afraid to ask for help from reliable sources so you can give your child the best diet possible.

One more important thing to note is that food manufacturers tend to change their production methods and ingredients regularly. This means you shouldn't feel complacent with products you have been buying for a long time. You should still read the labels of these products to ensure they fit into your child's diet. If you see any changes, especially the addition of gluten, it's time to find a healthier and safer replacement.

PROMOTE THE DIET THROUGH SOCIAL MEDIA

Social media has become such an important aspect of our lives. No matter where you look, social media is there. If you want to find something, you turn to social media. If you want to communicate with others, social media platforms make things easier. Unfortunately, this means that negativity can also spread like wildfire through social media. For instance, a lot of people don't take food sensitivities seriously. Although those who suffer from celiac disease know how serious it is, other people have a misconception that this disease isn't something to worry about. On the other hand, if a person says that they have a condition like cancer or heart disease, they are taken very seriously.

As a parent, you don't want this negativity in your child's life, as it will make things more difficult for both of you. Just because your child needs a special kind of diet, this shouldn't be a reason for others to ridicule or scrutinize them. Sadly, this is one of the problems that come with social media. If you don't want your child to experience this, then you should do something about it.

Since you can't get rid of social media, learn to use it to your advantage. For instance, if you see something on social media that either ridicules celiac disease or presents it in a negative light, get rid of it. Close the browser, move on to the next website, or simply hide the post. If it's really offensive, you can even report these things so they don't cause harm to anyone else. Just because other people don't understand how serious celiac disease is doesn't mean that you should let them affect you or your child.

By taking the necessary steps to protect your child and educate those around you, perhaps you can make a positive influence on social media, even if it's a small change. Here are some ways for you to take advantage of social media as part of your child's journey into going gluten-free:

Stand up and be brave

When it comes to social media, those who succeed are the ones who aren't afraid to speak their minds. As a parent whose child suffers from celiac disease, don't be scared to speak up to educate those who don't know anything about it. Often, people ridicule things they don't understand. If you can spread the word about the reality of celiac disease and how much it can affect a person's health, this will help others understand why those who suffer from the disease need to follow a special diet. They are not just being 'picky' or 'difficult.'

Set realistic goals

Apart from reading this book, you can go online to find ways to use social media to encourage your child to follow a gluten-free diet for the sake of their health. Come up with a set of goals for how you will do this. For instance, you can make a list of all the social media platforms your child has accounts on. Then, you can find groups, pages, or communities on these platforms to share with your child. These goals will take time to achieve, but at least you will be helping your child in a relevant and interesting way.

Work together with the people closest to your child

To improve your likelihood of success, ask for help and support from the people around your child, including their teacher and the rest of your household. Although you don't have to encourage everyone in your home to go gluten-free, especially if they don't need to, the least they can do is show their love and support to your child. The same thing goes at school. As mentioned, have a conversation with your child's teacher about their new diet. With all the support coming from those around you, both you and your child will feel more positive about this new endeavor.

Join or start a support group

Have you ever tried joining a support group? Support groups are a wonderful way to meet new people who are going through the same challenges as you. Through support groups, you can talk to other parents who are also helping their children transition to a gluten-free diet. You can share your experiences, ask for advice, or even share your own knowledge with other parents. This is another way to gain support, but this time coming from people you don't know. Go online and find groups to join. If you cannot find any local support groups, you can start your own. You can even look for support groups for your child. Just make sure to monitor your child's online activity to ensure that they are only discussing safe and relevant topics to help them accept their disease and adjust to their new diet.

Have a backup plan

At some point, you will experience challenges and setbacks—and these are okay. These are normal parts of the process. To deal with challenges, you may want to come up with a backup plan. For instance, if you see that your child's social media network isn't as positive as you had hoped, then you can think of ways to spread awareness about celiac disease. Or, if you discover that the support group your child has joined isn't educational at all, find another group. Having a backup plan makes you more confident about your child's gluten-free journey.

Try not to get discouraged

Sometimes, even your backup plans will fail. This is normal, too. Trust me. As someone who has successfully transitioned into a gluten-free life, I know all about these failures and challenges. The key here is to keep going. Learn from your mistakes and help your child move forward, too, by always being there to support them. After all, there is only so much you can do for your child. In the end, they should learn how to rise up and face challenges on their own.

Part of your child's journey is learning to deal with their social life as they go gluten-free. Explain that some people might not understand their diet and, because of this, they might be teased or taunted. This is especially true if nobody else follows the same diet. For instance, if your child is the only person in their class who suffers from celiac disease and needs to follow the gluten-free diet, they might feel isolated from their peers—even more so when your child goes online and doesn't see anything about celiac disease or the gluten-free diet.

So, what can you do?

Keep encouraging your child. The steps you will take to support your child will depend on their age and personality.

If your child has a lot of friends and loves to spend time on social media platforms, use this to encourage them. On the other hand, if your child is a bit of a loner and is very quiet, you can find other ways to help them out. It's all about spreading the right message and helping your child overcome the pressures of social media and their peers. If you can do that, you have already achieved some level of success... so keep going!

HELP YOUR CHILD TRANSITION TO THE GLUTEN-FREE DIET

After preparing yourself to help your child and preparing your child's surroundings, it is now time to focus on your child. To empower your child to follow a gluten-free diet for the rest of their lives, you must guide them until they understand what they need to do to succeed. Here are some things to help you out:

Start at Home

When you receive that devastating diagnosis from your child's doctor, try not to feel discouraged. Although it's normal to feel bad, you now understand how you can make things better for your child. Since your child spends most of their time at home, this is where you should start. Transitioning to a gluten-free diet doesn't just involve the foods they eat. Instead, you must also focus on all other aspects of your home. Here are the things you should do:

- Clean all of the cabinets where you will store your child's food. Also, label everything, especially if you live in a home with other people.
- Clean your kitchen appliances before using them to prepare your child's gluten-free meals.
- Check your child's health and personal products to make sure that they are gluten-free, too.
- Explain to your child where all of the gluten-free foods and snacks are stored so they know where to look when they feel hungry.

Also, educate the rest of your household about your child's new diet. Make sure they understand what your child is allowed and not allowed to eat. Also, encourage them to show support to your child so that they won't feel isolated at home.

Set Goals

Create goals for yourself and your child as part of your plans. For instance, you can eliminate foods that contain gluten gradually by creating a realistic schedule. Then you can create long-term goals for your child to achieve too. This will help keep both of you motivated to keep moving forward

Be a Good Role Model

If you can follow the diet along with your child, they will understand that it doesn't have to be a challenge. Whip up amazing gluten-free recipes for your child and enjoy these with them. Once in a while, encourage the rest of your household to share these meals, too. With you being a good role model, the transition won't seem as overwhelming to your child. Over time, they will see that this diet is their "new normal" and it isn't something to feel ashamed of.

Boost Your Child's Self-Esteem

Among all the people around your child, you are the one who has the most power to boost their self-esteem. Use this to your advantage as you guide your child. The more confident your child feels about going gluten-free, the more willing they will be to stick with the diet. Some ways to boost your child's self-esteem are:

- By encouraging and praising them genuinely.
- By using a positive approach when speaking with your child.
- By telling them that you are proud of them.
- By allowing your child to express themselves,

especially when things get tough.
- By avoiding criticism that sounds like shame or ridicule.

Celebrate Successes and Anticipate Challenges

Speaking of boosting your child's self-esteem, you can do this by celebrating successes no matter how small. Remember, you are taking this journey together. Going gluten-free isn't something that your child will do on their own. You should be there to guide them. And every time your child achieves something—like if they are able to stay away from gluten for a whole week—celebrate this! Such actions will make your child feel inspired and motivated.

Also, anticipate challenges so you are prepared whenever they come. This is where your backup plans come in. Simply knowing that you have a plan for when challenges come your way will make you feel better. And if you don't have to use those backup plans, it means that you and your child have successfully worked together to follow a specialized diet that will improve their health and keep them away from harm.

Teach Your Child to Navigate the World

When your child steps out of your home, they still have to follow a gluten-free diet. After you have established your home as a "safe zone," it's time to show your child how to navigate the rest of the world. Do this through social media, through your child's school, and through the other people in your child's life.

Empower your child by showing them that they can also follow their diet even when you're not around. Help your child come up with their own plan for how to deal with the outside world. And whenever your child comes home, ask them about their day and how they managed to stick with their diet. This will give you more opportunities to celebrate successes and boost your child's self-esteem.

Encourage Your Child to Explore

After your child learns how to navigate the world, the next thing you should do is encourage them to try new things. By this time, your child should have already gotten used to their diet. The next step is to learn to be more adventurous. This will make your child's gluten-free diet more interesting and, ultimately, more sustainable, too. To make this easier and more fun, look for opportunities to try new things together!

Awaken Your Child's Passion

As your child explores more gluten-free food options, they will discover that they are more passionate about certain foods than others. Give your child the freedom to choose what they eat. For instance, if they have a phase where they only want to eat fruits, let them. As long as the food they choose fits into their diet, allow your child to indulge. This is also the perfect time to introduce the importance of finding the right balance. For instance, if your child is all about fruits, introduce fruits that contain different types of nutrients. It's all about being creative to ensure a healthy and balanced diet.

Involve Your Child in the Process

Have you ever tried meal planning? This is an amazing process that can help increase your child's chances of success on a gluten-free diet. Meal planning involves taking the time to sit down, plan out your meals (usually for a week), and choosing a day to prepare and cook all of those meals. That way, you will always have meals ready for breakfast, lunch, dinner, and snacks. Meal planning can be a lot of fun, and if you involve your child in the process, they will learn how to become a master meal planner. This is a very useful skill for when they grow up.

Show Your Love and Support

Finally, and most importantly, show your love and support throughout the process. Let your child know that you will always be there to support them no matter what challenges come their way. If your child knows this, they will feel braver and more confident in their ability to make this diet a permanent part of their lives.

EMPOWER YOUR CHILD FOR THE FUTURE

Helping your child transition to a gluten-free diet is what you have to deal with right now, in the present. But this isn't enough. You should also help your child learn how to sustain this diet into adulthood. After all, the gluten-free diet will help them manage their condition so it doesn't worsen over time. Before moving on to the recipes, here are some final tips to help your child succeed in the future:

Educate your child

Until your child fully understands their condition and how important the diet is for them, they won't learn how to accept it. Educating your child is a process—it isn't something you can do in a day. As you do new things and take new steps throughout your child's journey, introduce new information about their diet. This way of educating your child is far more effective than trying to lecture them about why they should follow what you say.

Teach your child to be responsible for themselves

Being responsible is something we all do as adults. Right now, you can guide and help your child stick with the gluten-free diet. But when they grow up, you won't always be there to do this. Therefore, it's important to teach your child to be responsible enough to follow the diet. For instance, if your child forgets their lunchbox at home and they had to eat something at school that isn't gluten-free, they will probably experience uncomfortable or even painful symptoms when they get home. Take this opportunity to explain the importance of being responsible enough to remember their lunch box. Whenever things like this happen, make them into opportunities for your child to learn.

Help your child learn to read and understand food labels

It is important for you to learn how to read food labels properly and understand everything on them. That way, you can teach your child how to do the same. This is very important, especially as they start shopping for themselves in the future.

Teach your child to be creative

Apart from learning to be more adventurous, you should encourage your child to unleash their creativity to be more successful with their diet. For instance, if your child wants to try a new recipe, let them! If they need help, provide it. The more creative your child is, the more they will have fun with their diet.

Make it fun!

Speaking of having fun, another way to make this diet more sustainable is by creating good memories from the start. While your child is still young, introduce the gluten-free diet in fun and innovative ways. This will give your child good memories of the diet instead of remembering how you forced them to stop eating bread or other food items that they are fond of. Play games, watch videos, cook together, and more. Making this diet fun is easy if you unleash your own creativity, too.

Encourage your child to be proud of their diet

Although you cannot force your child to accept their diet and be proud of it, you can encourage this by being proud of the diet, too. Talk about it in a positive way all the time. If your child looks up to celebrities, find out which celebrities are following this diet. You can encourage your child to feel proud of their diet by associating it with the things they are most interested in.

Empower your child with "power statements"

Power statements are simple phrases or sentences that your child can say to themselves whenever they are feeling isolated or challenged. These power statements will also help your child develop their self-esteem. Here are some examples of power statements you can share with your child:

- Going gluten-free is the best choice for me!
- By avoiding gluten, I am helping my body heal.
- I may enjoy gluten, but I love myself more.
- I don't need gluten.
- The gluten-free diet is awesome just like me!

You can come up with your own power statements that you know will speak to your child and make them feel empowered.

Prepare them for social events

At some point, your child will have to attend parties and other social gatherings. These can be very challenging, especially since such gatherings usually involve sharing a meal. While your child is still young, show them how to carry themselves at parties. Politely ask the host ahead of time if there will be any gluten-free options served. If there aren't any planned, you can volunteer to bring at least one dish to share with all the other guests. If someone offers you food that contains gluten, politely decline and explain that you cannot eat gluten. By modeling these things, your child will learn how to attend parties without feeling stressed.

Encourage them to show appreciation

Whenever people try to accommodate your child's diet, show appreciation to them. This is very important, especially when your child grows up. While there were those who may ridicule and taunt, there were also those who will show kindness and support. These are the kinds of people you want your child to be around. And when such people show care and positivity, encourage your child to show them their gratitude and appreciation.

Help them transition into their "new normal"

As we all try to get used to the "new normal" because of the global pandemic, you can borrow this idea and use it for your child's transition. The gluten-free diet will be your child's lifelong diet, so they should get used to it. Keep encouraging your child until they come to accept the diet as their new normal. If you can do this, you will know that your child will succeed even as an adult.

Ultimately, your child must learn how to make healthy dietary choices for the sake of their own health and well-being. Your role as a parent is to encourage your child to learn all these things so that they can grow up into a well-rounded and confident adult. And one of the best things you can do for your child throughout this process is to create healthy and inspiring meals and snacks for them. Read on to learn how!

4

BREAKFAST RECIPES FOR THE WIN!

Have you ever heard the common saying about breakfast being the most important meal of the day? This is very true, especially for kids. Imagine how your child will feel if you send them off to school without breakfast. Chances are, they won't have the energy to learn and play with their classmates. Even if your child is following a gluten-free diet, you should still make sure that they eat regularly throughout the day—starting with a healthy and filling breakfast. In this chapter, we'll focus on the importance of breakfast with a number of amazing recipes you can whip up for your child.

THE MOST IMPORTANT MEAL OF THE DAY

When your child goes to sleep at night, they start a long fasting period as they won't be eating anything after dinner (unless you give your child a nighttime snack). When your child wakes up in the morning, they wouldn't have eaten anything for more than eight hours! As your child eats breakfast, they are "breaking their fast" and giving their body the fuel it needs to function well. While some adults skip breakfast as part of their diets, this isn't recommended for children. For young ones, breakfast is important as it offers the following benefits:

- To give your child the energy they need throughout the morning
- To give them a boost of brainpower
- To increase their intake of the recommended essential nutrients each day
- To reduce their risk of developing certain illnesses
- ... and so much more

Breakfast should be a part of your child's morning routine no matter how busy your mornings are as a family. Fortunately, there are a lot of easy and quick gluten-free breakfast dishes you can whip up for your child, some of which you will learn later on.

TRY NOT TO OVERDO IT!

Whenever you have breakfast, what do you usually eat? If you're like most adults (yes, even parents), a cup of coffee and a piece of toast usually constitutes their breakfast. Of course, a breakfast this simple isn't ideal for growing children. As a parent, you can use each of your child's meals as an opportunity to help them learn how to make healthy food choices. There are so many great options for those who follow gluten-free diets that you won't run out of dishes to serve. But when it comes to serving breakfast to your child, you should also be careful not to overdo it.

Right now, you might be thinking, "How do I overdo breakfast?"

Before we go through that, you should first know what may happen to your child when you overdo breakfast. Usually, when someone eats a large meal for breakfast, it makes them feel sleepy instead of giving them a boost of energy. If you give your child a huge meal, they will feel too relaxed, and keeping their eyes open will be a struggle. Of course, this isn't ideal if you are sending your child off to school after breakfast.

Yes, the body needs food for energy. But after a huge meal, when the body starts breaking down food, many things happen. Interestingly enough, one of the things that happens is drowsiness. The main reason for this is that some hormone levels change, specifically those of serotonin and melanin, and these changes make us feel sleepy. Because of this, it's recommended to serve the proper portions to your child, without making them feel restricted.

In other words, as important as breakfast is, you don't want your child to eat so much that they end up feeling sluggish all morning. Apart from the amount of food your child eats for breakfast, you should also watch what your child is eating. Choose ingredients that are healthy and good for their gut, brain, and all other bodily functions. This means that your child should follow a healthy, balanced diet that includes whole grains, fruits, veggies, fatty fish, and high-fiber carbs. Also, you should avoid giving your child too much sugar, as this might cause them to have a sugar crash later in the day.

Feeding your child a healthy breakfast each day will make them energized and capable. Pair this with a good night's sleep and your child will surely feel happy from morning until night. A nutritious and filling breakfast will give your child's metabolism a boost, improve their cognitive function, give them plenty of energy, and reduce cravings where they might reach for unhealthy snacks while at school.

The bottom line is this: after eating a healthy breakfast, your child will feel energized, excited, and ready for whatever may come their way. To achieve all of these wonderful effects, you can start with these healthy, tasty, and fun breakfast recipes that fit right into your child's diet, because they're gluten-free!

SWEET POTATO SMOOTHIE BOWL

There's nothing more colorful and interesting than a smoothie bowl. Prepare this nourishing dish that offers a combination of warm flavors from the sweet potato and pumpkin spice. This is a quick and easy recipe that you can use as a basis for different types of gluten-free smoothie bowls in the future.

Time: 5 minutes

Serving Size: 1 serving

Prep Time: 5 minutes

Cook Time: no cooking time

Ingredients:

- ⅛ tsp nutmeg (ground)
- ¼ tsp ginger (ground)
- ½ tsp cinnamon (ground)
- ½ tsp vanilla extract
- 2 tbsp maple syrup
- ¼ cup of grain-free oats
- ¾ cup of sweet potato (puréed)
- 1 cup of almond milk
- Cloves (just a pinch)
- Sliced fruits (let your child choose)
- Chia granola (optional)

Directions:

1. In a blender, add all of the ingredients except for the sliced fruits and chia granola.
2. Blend everything until you get a smooth texture.
3. Pour the smoothie into a bowl.
4. Top with sliced fruits and chia granola if using, then serve right away.

POWER BREAKFAST BOWL

Breakfast bowls are easy, healthy, and filling. Surely, this one will give your child all the energy they need for school, play, and much more. It contains healthy, gluten-free ingredients that are tasty and nourishing, too. This is another customizable recipe where you can easily swap out ingredients based on your child's preferences.

Time: 15 minutes

Serving Size: 1 serving

Prep Time: 5 minutes

Cook Time: 10 minutes

Ingredients:

- 2 tsp seeds or nuts (let your child choose)
- ¼ cup of non-dairy milk (vanilla flavored or plain)
- ½ cup of plain quinoa (cooked)
- ½ cup of sliced fruits (let your child choose)
- 1 tsp maple syrup (if you aren't using sweetened milk)
- Cardamom, cinnamon, or nutmeg (just a pinch to taste)

Directions:

1. In a saucepan, add the milk and quinoa, then mix well.
2. Warm the mixture until the quinoa absorbs the milk.
3. When most of the milk has been absorbed by the quinoa, transfer the mixture to a bowl.
4. Add the spices and maple syrup (if using), then mix well.
5. Top with sliced fruits and nuts or seeds, and serve!

SAVORY CREPES

Most kids love sweet crepes, but have you ever tried serving savory crepes to your little one? Here's an interesting recipe for your child's breakfast routine. It's packed with healthy ingredients and an amazing combination of flavors. Of course, you can change the filling ingredients, too... you can even give your child a choice!

Time: 15 minutes

Serving Size: 4 to 6 servings (depending on the size of the crepes)

Prep Time: 5 minutes

Cook Time: 10 minutes

Ingredients for the crepes:

- ¼ tsp sea salt
- 1 tbsp butter (melted then cooled)
- 1 tbsp honey
- ½ cup of oat flour
- ½ cup of whole milk
- 2 large eggs
- Cooking spray

Ingredients for the savory filling:

- 2 tbsp basil (minced)
- ½ cup of goat cheese (room temperature)
- 12 tomato slices

Directions:

1. In a bowl, combine all of the crepe ingredients and whisk well until you get a smooth texture.
2. Lightly grease a skillet with cooking spray. Pour around ¼ cup of batter in the skillet, then tilt the skillet around to spread the batter.

3. Cook each crepe for about 30 to 45 seconds, flip, and continue cooking for about 15 more seconds.
4. Once done, transfer the crepe to a plate and continue cooking crepes until you've used up all of the batter.
5. Spread goat cheese on one of the crepes, then top with 3 slices of tomato and a sprinkle of basil.
6. Fold the crepe in half and put it back into the skillet.
7. Cook for about 30 seconds or so then flip over and cook for another 30 seconds.
8. Transfer the crepe to a plate and continue assembling and cooking the other crepes.
9. Serve while hot!

CINNAMON TOAST BREAKFAST MUFFINS

These breakfast muffins are fluffy, moist, and buttery. Your child will surely enjoy every single bite while feeling nourished by these protein-rich treats they can also be served as a filling snack. You may want to bake more than one batch because the rest of your family will love these muffins, too!

Time: 30 minutes

Serving Size: 12 muffins

Prep Time: 10 minutes

Cook Time: 20 minutes

Ingredients for the muffins:

- ½ tsp apple cider vinegar
- ½ tsp salt
- ½ tsp vanilla extract
- 2 tsp cinnamon
- 1 tbsp baking powder
- 2 tbsp oat flour
- ½ cup of butter (melted)
- 1 cup of coconut sugar
- 1 ⅓ cups of silken tofu (non-GMO, organic)
- 2 cups of oat flour
- Cooking spray

Ingredients for the topping:

- ¼ tbsp cinnamon (powdered)
- ¾ tbsp sugar (powdered)

Directions:

1. Preheat your oven to 400 F and use cooking spray to grease a muffin tin.

2. In a small bowl, combine the topping ingredients, mix well, and set aside.
3. In a bowl, mix together the cinnamon, baking powder, oat flour, and salt. Set aside.
4. In a blender, add the apple cider vinegar, coconut sugar, butter, vanilla extract, and tofu, then blend until you get a smooth texture.
5. Pour the mixture into the bowl with the dry ingredients and mix well until you form a batter.
6. Transfer the batter to the greased muffin pan.
7. Top each muffin with the cinnamon sugar.
8. Place the muffin pan in the oven for about 12 minutes.
9. Lower the heat to 350 F and continue baking for 8 more minutes.
10. Take the pan out of the oven and allow the muffins to cool down before serving.

MORNING MAC & CHEESE

Mac & cheese for breakfast? This will delight your child. Although this dish is usually served for lunch or dinner, it can also make for a fun, healthy, and tasty breakfast. It's cheesy, creamy, and oh-so-satisfying. Whip up this big batch and enjoy it with your child!

Time: 50 minutes

Serving Size: 8 servings

Prep Time: 20 minutes

Cook Time: 30 minutes

Ingredients:

- ½ tsp dry mustard
- 1 tsp salt
- 3 tbsp brown rice flour
- 3 tbsp olive oil
- ½ cup of dry bread crumbs (gluten-free)
- 1 cup of breakfast sausage (browned, crumbled, you can also use cooked ham or bacon)
- 2 cups of cheddar cheese (shredded)
- 2 cups of dry macaroni (gluten-free, cooked)
- 2 cups of whole milk
- 3 large eggs

Directions:

1. Preheat your oven to 350 F and use cooking spray to grease a baking dish.
2. In a saucepan, warm the olive oil over medium heat.
3. Add the flour and whisk for about 5 minutes, making sure that it doesn't brown.
4. Whisk in the milk, mustard powder, and salt. Continue whisking until no lumps remain.
5. Allow the mixture to simmer for 5 to 10 minutes or until it thickens.
6. Turn off the heat and remove the pan.
7. In a bowl, add the eggs and ¼ cup of the milk mixture, then whisk gently.
8. Add half of the cheese and continue whisking to combine.
9. Add the sausage to the cheese sauce and mix well.
10. Add the cooked macaroni to the cheese sauce and continue mixing until everything is well incorporated.
11. Pour the mac & cheese mixture into the baking dish.
12. In a bowl, combine the breadcrumbs and the remaining cheese.
13. Sprinkle the mixture over the mac & cheese.

14. Place the baking dish in the oven and bake for about 30 minutes.
15. Take the baking dish out of the oven and allow to cool slightly before serving.

CLASSIC BLUEBERRY MUFFINS

When you think about muffins, you're probably picturing the classic blueberry muffin in your mind. This recipe is quick, easy, tasty, and gluten-free. If your child craves something sweet in the morning, and you'd rather they eat something healthy, this is an amazing option. You can even freeze the rest and reheat the next morning.

Time: 40 minutes

Serving Size: 12 muffins

Prep Time: 15 minutes

Cook Time: 25 minutes

Ingredients for the muffins:

- ½ tsp baking soda
- ½ tsp sea salt
- ¼ cup of butter (unsalted, room temperature)
- ½ cup of arrowroot flour

- ½ cup of coconut flour (sifted)
- ½ cup of honey (preferably the runny variety)
- 1 ½ cups of blueberries (fresh or frozen)
- 6 large eggs
- Cooking spray

Ingredients for the almond crumble:

- ⅛ tsp cinnamon (ground)
- ⅛ tsp sea salt
- ¼ cup of butter (unsalted, room temperature)
- ¼ cup of coconut sugar (granulated)
- ½ cup of almond flour
- ½ cup of arrowroot flour

Directions:

1. Preheat your oven to 350 F and use cooking spray to grease a muffin pan.
2. In a bowl, add the arrowroot flour, coconut flour, baking soda, and sea salt, then mix to combine.
3. Sift the dry ingredients together and set aside.
4. In a stand or electric mixer, add the honey and butter, then blend until you get a creamy consistency.
5. Add the eggs to the mixer and continue blending

until even.

6. Add the dry ingredients into the mixer and continue blending until smooth.
7. Fold the blueberries into the mixture, then set aside for about 5 minutes to thicken.
8. While the batter is resting, add the ingredients for the almond crumble into a bowl.
9. Mix until the crumble starts sticking together and forming clumps.
10. Transfer the batter into the greased muffin pan, topping each muffin with the almond crumble mixture.
11. Place the muffin pan into the oven and bake for about 25 minutes.
12. Take the muffin pan out of the oven and allow to cool completely before serving.

MEDITERRANEAN QUICHES

These Mediterranean quiches are wonderfully flaky and have a unique flavor. In this recipe, you will be using fresh ingredients for a healthy, filling, and yummy breakfast your child will enjoy. Although this dish does take some time to prepare, all your efforts will be worth it as your child will appreciate and enjoy these quiches you will serve.

Time: 1 hour and 30 minutes

Serving Size: 12 mini quiches

Prep Time: 30 minutes

Cook Time: 1 hour

Ingredients for the crust:

- ½ tsp salt
- ¾ tsp baking soda
- 1 ½ tbsp water
- ¾ cup of coconut oil (melted)
- 2 cups of almond flour

Ingredients for the filling:

- 2 tbsp vegetable broth (you can also use nut or seed milk)
- ¼ cup of nutritional yeast
- ½ cup of red olives (pitted, sliced)
- ½ cup of sun-dried tomatoes (sliced)
- ½ red onion (finely diced)
- 2 cloves of garlic
- 2 handfuls of baby spinach (chopped)
- 4 eggs (preferably organic)
- Black pepper
- Salt

Directions:

1. Preheat your oven to 350 F and use cooking spray to grease a muffin tin.
2. In a bowl, add the baking soda, almond flour, and salt, then whisk well.
3. Add ½ cup of the coconut oil and the water, then continue mixing. As you mix, gradually add the rest of the coconut oil while the mixture is coming together. You know that you are done when you have a crumbly crust that is sticky enough to hold together.
4. Spoon the crust into the greased muffin tin and press it down to form the shape of the mini quiche crusts. Cover the whole bottom and halfway up along the sides.
5. Use a toothpick to poke holes in the bottom of the crusts.
6. Place the muffin tin into the oven and bake the crusts for about 10 to 15 minutes.
7. While baking the crust, add the onions into a pan and sauté over medium heat for about 5 minutes.
8. Add the garlic and continue sautéing for about 2 more minutes until fragrant.
9. Add the baby spinach and continue sautéing for about 5 more minutes until wilted.

10. Take the pan off of the stove.
11. Add the olives and sun-dried tomatoes, toss to combine, then set aside.
12. In a bowl, add the eggs, nutritional yeast, vegetable stock, salt, and pepper, and beat until frothy.
13. When the crust is done, take the muffin tin out of the oven.
14. Pour the Mediterranean mixture into each of the mini quiches.
15. Top each mini quiche with the egg mixture.
16. Place the muffin tin back into the oven and continue baking the quiches for 20 to 40 minutes. If you are using mini muffin tins, 20 to 30 minutes will be sufficient. But if you're using regular-sized muffin tins, you may have to wait up to 40 minutes. You want the quiches to be cooked all the way through. You can insert a toothpick into one of your quiches to check if they're done.
17. Once cooked, take the muffin tin out of the oven and allow the quiches to cool before serving.

COOKIES FOR BREAKFAST!

These healthy and hearty cookies taste incredible and you can have them ready in half an hour. They're easy to make and when you tell your child that they will be having cookies for breakfast, watch as their face lights up!

Time: 30 minutes

Serving Size: 12 cookies

Prep Time: 14 minutes

Cook Time: 16 minutes

Ingredients:

- ½ tsp salt
- 1 tsp cinnamon (ground)
- ¼ cup of maple syrup (you can also use honey)
- ⅓ cup of apple butter (store-bought or homemade)
- ½ cup of pumpkin seeds
- ½ cup of cranberries (dried)
- ½ cup of raisins
- 1 cup of almond butter (you can also use peanut butter or any kind of seed butter)
- 2 cups of quick oats (you can also use old-fashioned whole oats)
- 1 large banana (mashed)

Directions:

1. Preheat your oven to 325 F and use parchment paper to line a large baking sheet.
2. In a bowl, add all of the ingredients, and use a hand mixer to combine everything until you get a heavy, thick dough.
3. Take a portion of the dough, roll it into a ball, and place it on the baking sheet. Use your palm to flatten the cookie slightly. Repeat until you have used up all of the dough to make cookies.
4. Place the baking sheet into the oven and bake the cookies for 16 to 18 minutes. The cooking time depends on the size of the cookies.
5. Take the baking sheet out of the oven and allow them to cool down completely before serving.

SAVORY OAT BOWL

With this savory bowl of oats, you can transform your child's delicious breakfast into a hearty meal. It's a colorful dish that takes only minutes to make. It's perfect for those busy mornings when everyone is in a rush, but you still want your child to eat something healthy and delicious in the morning.

Time: 10 minutes

Serving Size: 2 servings

Prep Time: 5 minutes

Cook Time: 5 minutes

Ingredients:

- ⅛ tsp black pepper
- ½ tsp sea salt
- 2 tsp olive oil
- 3 tbsp nutritional yeast
- 1 cup grape tomatoes (each cut in half)
- 1 cup of oats (preferably organic)
- 2 cups of water
- 1 small avocado (pitted, sliced)
- 1 handful of baby spinach (you can also use arugula or baby kale)

Directions:

1. In a saucepan, add the oats and water over medium-high heat and bring to a boil.
2. Once boiling, turn the heat down and allow to simmer for 3 to 5 minutes until you achieve the desired texture.
3. Add the oil, nutritional yeast, salt, and black pepper, and mix well.

4. Spoon the cooked oats into serving bowls and top with avocado, baby spinach, and tomatoes.
5. Serve while hot.

CHOCOLATE CHIP PANCAKES WITH OATS

These pancakes are filling, nutritious, and super moist. Since they also have chocolate chips, your child will surely enjoy them. One of the best things about these pancakes is that they're not too sweet. When your child has these pancakes for breakfast, they will start the day feeling happy and satisfied.

Time: 25 minutes

Serving Size: 2 servings

Prep Time: 15 minutes

Cook Time: 10 minutes

Ingredients:

- 1 tsp baking powder
- 1 tbsp almond butter
- 1 tbsp avocado oil (you can also use coconut oil)
- 2 tbsp almond meal
- 3 tbsp chocolate chips (semisweet, non-dairy)
- ¼ cup of all-purpose flour (gluten-free)
- ⅓ cup of almond milk (unsweetened, you can also use other types of nut milk)
- ½ cup of rolled oats (gluten-free)
- 1 flax egg (mix 3 tbsp of water and 1 tbsp of ground flaxseed meal then allow to thicken in the refrigerator for at least 15 minutes)
- 1 medium banana (very ripe, mashed)
- Cooking spray
- Salt
- ½ tsp vanilla extract (optional)
- 1 tsp maple or agave syrup (optional)

Directions:

1. In a bowl, add the banana, baking powder, and flax egg. Mix well.
2. Add the almond milk, almond butter, oil, salt, and vanilla extract if desired, then mix until well combined.
3. Add the almond meal, oats, and flour. Continue mixing until the ingredients are just combined.
4. Gently fold the chocolate chips into the mixture and allow to rest for about 5 minutes.
5. Preheat your griddle over medium-low heat.
6. Pour the pancake batter into the griddle and spread to the desired size.
7. Cook the pancake for 3 to 4 minutes, then flip it over. Continue cooking for 3 to 4 more minutes until golden brown.
8. Once cooked, transfer the pancake to a plate and continue cooking the rest of the pancakes until you finish all of the batter.
9. Serve warm with a drizzle of maple syrup and more chocolate chips if desired.

GOOD MORNING BURRITO

If you have any leftover taco meat in your refrigerator, you can use it to make this super easy dish. Of course, you can also cook a fresh batch and store any leftovers in the fridge for other yummy recipes. For now, you can spice up your child's breakfast with this healthy treat.

Time: 20 minutes

Serving Size: 1 serving

Prep Time: 10 minutes

Cook Time: 10 minutes

Ingredients:

- ½ tsp garlic powder
- 1 tsp coconut oil
- 1 tsp cumin
- 1 tsp onion powder
- 3 tbsp guacamole (store-bought or homemade)
- ⅛ cup of red onion (julienned)
- ⅛ cup of salsa (store-bought or homemade)
- ¼ lb ground beef (you can also use ground turkey)
- 3 eggs
- Black pepper
- Salt
- 1 tsp cilantro (optional, for garnish)
- 1 tsp paprika (optional)

Directions:

1. In a skillet, add the ground beef over medium heat and cook until browned.
2. Once browned, add the garlic powder, cumin, onion powder, salt, pepper, and paprika if desired. Mix well, then set aside.
3. In a bowl, add the eggs and whisk well.
4. In a pan, warm the coconut oil over medium-low heat.
5. Pour the eggs into the pan and spread into a thin and even layer.
6. Cook the eggs slowly for about 6 minutes without flipping.
7. Once cooked, slide the eggs onto a plate.
8. Transfer the seasoned meat onto the eggs and top with salsa, guacamole, and onion.
9. Sprinkle with cilantro, if desired, and serve while hot.

SUPER-POWERED CHIA PUDDING

This recipe combines chia seeds and oats to give your child a super-powered start to the day. If you want your child to feel full the whole morning while still having the energy to do everything they need to, this dish is a winner. The best part is, it's super easy to make!

Time: 5 minutes (plus chilling time)

Serving Size: 1 serving

Prep Time: 5 minutes

Cook Time: no cooking time

Ingredients for the pudding:

- 1 tbsp cherries (dried)
- 1 tbsp maple syrup
- 1 tbsp pumpkin seeds
- 2 tbsp oats
- ¼ cup of chia seeds
- 1 ½ cups of oat milk (or preferred type of milk)
- ½ apple (grated)

Ingredients for the topping:

- Cherries (frozen)
- Pumpkin seeds

Directions:

1. In a bowl, add all of the pudding ingredients and whisk vigorously.
2. Cover the bowl with a sheet of cling wrap and place in the refrigerator for at least an hour.

3. Before serving, stir the pudding until free of clumps and top with pumpkin seeds, cherries, and any other desired topping.

SWEET POTATO FRENCH TOAST

French toast is a classic breakfast dish, but while your child is on a gluten-free diet, bread is a no-no. So it's up to you to come up with creative dishes to keep your child healthy and interested—and this is one such dish. Here, you will be using gluten-free bread, which makes this recipe suitable for your child's new diet.

Time: 35 minutes

Serving Size: 2 servings

Prep Time: 5 minutes

Cook Time: 30 minutes

Ingredients:

- ⅛ tsp cinnamon
- ½ tsp vanilla extract
- 1 tsp maple syrup (you can also use raw honey)
- ½ cup of sweet potato (cooked, puréed)
- ¾ cup of milk

- 4 eggs
- 4 slices of bread (gluten-free)
- Nutmeg
- Sea salt
- Butter (for cooking)

Directions:

1. In a bowl, add the maple syrup, sweet potato purée, milk, eggs, and vanilla extract. Whisk well, until you reach a thin consistency. If it's too thick, you may add more milk.
2. Add the cinnamon, along with a dash of nutmeg and salt, then mix to combine.
3. In a pan, melt some butter over medium heat.
4. Once hot, dip one slice of bread in the batter and place into the pan.
5. Fry one side for about 4 minutes until golden brown. Flip over and fry the other side for about 3 to 4 minutes until golden brown.
6. Once cooked, transfer the French toast to a plate.
7. Repeat the cooking steps for the rest of the bread slices.
8. Serve while hot!

BREKKIE PIZZA

Pizza for breakfast? Yes, please! Here's a fun dish that your child will enjoy for their first meal of the day. It's made with a cauliflower crust, which is yummy and healthy, too. You can even mix and match the topping ingredients according to your child's preferences. Perfect!

Time: 50 minutes

Serving Size: 1 pizza

Prep Time: 10 minutes

Cook Time: 40 minutes

Ingredients:

- ⅛ tsp marjoram (fresh, chopped)
- ⅛ tsp olive oil
- ¼ tsp oregano (fresh, chopped)
- ¼ tsp salt
- ¼ tsp thyme (fresh, chopped)
- ¼ cup of Parmesan cheese (shredded)
- ¼ cup of pizza sauce (store-bought or homemade)
- ¾ cup of mozzarella cheese (shredded)
- 3 cups of cauliflower (florets only, rinsed)
- 3 eggs

- Pizza toppings of your choice

Directions:

1. Place the cauliflower florets in a food processor and pulse until finely chopped.
2. In a skillet, add the olive oil and cauliflower over medium-low heat. Cook for about 5 minutes until tender.
3. Transfer the cauliflower into a bowl lined with cheesecloth and allow to cool slightly.
4. Once cooled, tightly wrap the cauliflower with the cheesecloth to wring out as much water as you can. If you don't wring out enough water, you will end up with a soggy pizza crust so you shouldn't skip this step.
5. Preheat your oven to 400 F and use parchment paper to line a baking sheet.
6. In a bowl, mix together the cauliflower, salt, thyme, oregano, marjoram, ¼ cup of mozzarella cheese, and the Parmesan cheese.
7. Beat one of the eggs and add it to the crust mixture.
8. Use your hands to mix the dough. Once the dough has formed, divide it in half and roll each portion into a ball.
9. Use a rolling pin to flatten the dough balls, then

transfer to the baking sheet. You can also make one big pizza if you have a big enough baking sheet.
10. Place the baking sheet in the oven and bake the crusts for about 15 minutes.
11. Take the baking sheet out of the oven, then add pizza sauce to the crusts and spread evenly all the way to the edges. Top with the remaining mozzarella cheese.
12. Add the pizza toppings of your choice. As you add more toppings, use your fingers to make a well in the middle of each pizza.
13. Crack an egg into each of the wells you have made.
14. Place the baking sheet back into the oven and continue baking the pizzas for 15 minutes more.
15. Take the baking sheet out of the oven and allow the pizzas to cool down slightly before slicing and serving.

PEANUT BUTTER PANCAKES

Pancakes are a popular choice for breakfast, especially for kids. If you need a quick dish that's tasty and easy to prepare, this is an amazing option. These pancakes are filling, rich, all-natural, and sweet enough that you don't need syrup. Since these pancakes are flourless, they fit right into your child's gluten-free diet.

Time: 15 minutes

Serving Size: 4 servings

Prep Time: 5 minutes

Cook Time: 10 minutes

Ingredients:

- 1 ½ tsp baking powder
- 2 tbsp honey
- 1 cup of milk
- 1 cup of peanut butter (natural, creamy)
- 3 eggs
- Cooking spray (for cooking)

Directions:

1. In a bowl, combine all of the ingredients and whisk well.
2. Grease a skillet with cooking spray over low-medium heat. Don't heat the skillet up too much, as you might burn your pancakes.
3. Pour about ⅓ cup of batter into the skillet and allow to cook until the bottom turns golden brown.
4. Flip the pancake and cook the other side until it turns golden brown, too. You may insert a

toothpick to check if the pancake is done. If it comes out clean, you know it's cooked all the way to the center.

5. Once cooked, transfer the pancake to a plate.
6. Repeat the cooking steps until you have used up all of the batter.
7. Serve the pancakes warm with a side of sliced fruit or a drizzle of honey.

ITALIAN BAKE

This delicious dish is nutritious, lean, and oh-so-yummy. Although it takes an hour to prep and cook this recipe, it will definitely be worth the wait. Cook this dish on a lazy weekend morning so that you can enjoy it with your child as you share stories with the rest of the family.

Time: 1 hour

Serving Size: 4 servings

Prep Time: 5 minutes

Cook Time: 55 minutes

Ingredients:

- ¼ tsp black pepper

- ½ tsp basil (dried)
- ½ tsp salt
- ¼ cup of Parmesan cheese (grated)
- 4 cups of plum tomatoes (cut into chunks)
- 1 onion (sliced)
- 1 red bell pepper (sliced)
- 1 zucchini (cut into chunks)
- 2 large cloves of garlic (minced)
- 4 large eggs
- Cooking spray

Directions:

1. Preheat your oven to 400 F and grease a roasting pan with cooking spray.
2. Place the tomatoes, onion, red bell pepper, zucchini, garlic, basil, salt, and pepper in the roasting pan.
3. Toss lightly to coat with the cooking spray.
4. Place the roasting pan in the oven and cook the vegetables for about 30 minutes until tender and brown. While roasting, stir the veggies occasionally.
5. Once cooked, take the roasting pan out of the oven.
6. Grease 4 ramekins with cooking spray and spoon the roasted veggies into the ramekins.

7. Crack one egg over the roasted veggies in each ramekin and top with Parmesan cheese.
8. Place the ramekins on a baking sheet.
9. Place the baking sheet in the oven for about 25 minutes until the eggs are set.
10. Take the baking sheet out of the oven and allow the ramekins to cool down slightly before serving.

CLASSIC OATMEAL WITH CARAMELIZED BANANA

A bowl of oatmeal for breakfast is hearty, healthy, and comforting. This recipe offers a new twist to this classic dish with the addition of caramelized banana, melty chocolate, and crunchy granola. It's a perfect combination that will soon become one of your child's favorite breakfast dishes.

Time: 15 minutes

Serving Size: 2 servings

Prep Time: 5 minutes

Cook Time: 10 minutes

Ingredients:

- ½ tbsp coconut oil (you can also use butter)

- ½ tbsp molasses
- 1 tbsp brown sugar (divided)
- 2 tbsp dark chocolate (cut into chunks)
- ¼ cup of granola (gluten-free)
- ½ cup of oats
- 1 cup of water
- 1 banana (cut into thick pieces)
- Salt
- Almond milk (optional, for topping)

Directions:

1. In a skillet, warm the coconut oil over medium heat.
2. Add the banana slices and sprinkle with brown sugar.
3. Cook the banana slices for about 2 minutes until soft and golden brown, then flip them over.
4. Continue cooking for 2 minutes more until the other side has turned golden brown, too.
5. Transfer the caramelized banana slices to a plate then set aside.
6. In a saucepan, add the water, oats, molasses, and salt over medium heat.
7. Cook the oats for about 3 to 5 minutes, stirring often, until you have the consistency you desire.

8. Once cooked, pour the oatmeal into bowls.
9. Top with granola, caramelized banana, chocolate chunks, and almond milk if desired. Serve while hot.

BREAKFAST SALAD WITH GRILLED FRUITS

This is a unique dish that's simple, chic, and refreshing. When you serve this to your child, they might give you a surprised look. But once your child tastes this salad, they'll be begging you for more. The best part is, it's super healthy!

Time: 15 minutes

Serving Size: 2 servings

Prep Time: 5 minutes

Cook Time: 10 minutes

Ingredients for the coconut whip:

- ⅛ tsp cream of tartar
- 2 tbsp berry sugar (you can also use icing sugar)
- 1 ¾ cup of coconut cream (chilled overnight)

Ingredients for the salad:

- ½ tbsp coconut oil (melted)
- 1 tbsp agave nectar
- 1 banana (sliced lengthwise)
- 1 large peach (pitted, cut into quarters)
- 2 pineapple slices (cored)
- Chia seeds (for topping)
- Vegetable oil (for brushing the grill)

Directions:

1. Take the coconut cream out of the refrigerator and only scoop the thickest portion out. You may discard the remaining coconut water or save it for another recipe.
2. In a bowl, add the coconut cream, berry sugar, and cream of tartar.
3. Beat the mixture on high speed until you get an airy and thick texture.
4. Place the bowl in the refrigerator to chill until you need it.
5. In a bowl, mix together the agave nectar and coconut oil.
6. Preheat your grill and grease it lightly with vegetable oil.
7. Brush the syrup mixture over the fruit slices and place them on the grill.

8. Grill the fruit slices until caramelized, then flip them over and caramelize the other side.
9. When done, arrange the fruit slices on a plate.
10. Sprinkle the fruits with chia seeds and serve with the coconut whip for a refreshing breakfast treat.

COCO-BANANA WAFFLES

These waffles are chewy, sweet, and have a lovely crisp exterior. If your child is craving something other than pancakes, whip up these waffles for them. With their unique flavor, your child will appreciate this sweet treat that's super healthy, too.

Time: 40 minutes

Serving Size: 6 waffles

Prep Time: 10 minutes

Cook Time: 30 minutes

Ingredients:

- 1 tsp cinnamon (ground)
- 1 tsp vanilla extract
- ½ tbsp arrowroot powder
- 1 tbsp baking powder
- 2 tbsp chia seeds (ground, you can also use flax seeds)
- 2 tbsp maple syrup
- ¼ cup of coconut oil (melted)
- ¼ cup of sorghum flour (sweetened)
- ½ cup of coconut (unsweetened, shredded)
- 1 cup of almond meal (you can also use almond flour)
- 1 cup of oat flour
- 1 ¼ cups of non-dairy milk
- 1 large banana (mashed)
- Salt

Directions:

1. Preheat your waffle iron to the doneness setting you desire and use parchment paper to line a baking sheet.
2. Preheat your oven to 225 F. You can keep the

waffles warm here, or you can skip this step if desired.

3. In a bowl, add the banana, maple syrup, oil, vanilla extract, and chia seeds.
4. Whisk the ingredients together until well combined, then set aside.
5. In a separate bowl, mix together the oat flour, almond meal, baking powder, coconut, sorghum flour, cinnamon, and salt.
6. Stir the banana mixture one more time, then add it to the dry ingredient mixture.
7. Mix well until you get a batter-like consistency that's a bit stiff.
8. Open your waffle iron and use coconut oil to grease it lightly.
9. Pour about ½ a cup of batter into the middle of your waffle iron and close the lid.
10. Cook the waffle for about 4 minutes (the cooking time depends on your waffle maker).
11. Use a fork to gently remove the cooked waffle and transfer it to the baking sheet.
12. If desired, place the baking sheet in the oven to keep the waffle warm as you continue cooking the rest of the waffles.
13. After cooking all of the waffles, serve while warm.

Top the waffle with fresh fruit slices, maple syrup, and other toppings your child loves.

EGGY BREAKFAST CUPS

These super-powered egg cups are perfect for breakfast or for a healthy, filling snack. Each egg cup is loaded with lean protein, fiber, and amazing flavor. Although this recipe doesn't include meat, you can easily add turkey, chicken, or even bacon to make it more appealing to your child.

Time: 50 minutes

Serving Size: 12 breakfast cups

Prep Time: 10 minutes

Cook Time: 40 minutes

Ingredients:

- ¼ tsp garlic salt
- ¼ cup of onion (diced)
- ½ cup of cauliflower (diced)
- ½ cup of cheddar cheese (shredded, you can use any other type of cheese, too)
- 1 cup of bell peppers (diced)
- 1 cup of egg whites

- 2 cups of quinoa (cooked then cooled)
- 2 whole eggs
- ½ avocado (pitted, peeled, diced)
- Black pepper
- Cooking spray
- Salt

Directions:

1. Preheat your oven to 350 F and use cooking spray to grease a muffin tin.
2. In a bowl, add the egg white and eggs, then whisk until well combined.
3. Add the rest of the ingredients and mix well.
4. Scoop the egg cup mixture evenly into the muffin tins. If you have any leftover mixture, you may set it aside and cook another batch.
5. Place the muffin tin in the oven and bake the egg cups for about 40 minutes.
6. Once cooked, take the muffin tin out of the oven and allow the muffin tin to cool down completely.
7. Once cooled, remove the egg cups using a knife and serve while warm.

5

SNACKING LIKE A BOSS

A child's day isn't complete without snacks. Some children have a snack once a day, some have snacks twice a day, and others snack throughout the day. Although snacking too frequently isn't ideal, providing healthy snacks in the morning and in the afternoon will help your child feel happy and energized all day long. In this chapter, you will learn all about snacking, along with a number of healthy and yummy recipes you can start preparing for your child.

THE IMPORTANCE OF SNACKS

Children love snack time—for them, it's one of the most enjoyable meals of the day. If your child is asking you for a snack, it's better to prepare one for them instead of telling them to find a snack for themselves. Given such a choice, there is a very high chance that your child will opt for something that's too sweet, too salty, or generally unhealthy. Between regular meals, children have to eat healthy snacks, especially if they lead active lives. To maintain their energy throughout the day, your child needs to have a snack or two, preferably something healthy. When most adults hear the word 'snack,' they immediately think of something unhealthy or unnecessary. But for children, snacks are important for the following reasons:

- It provides your child with more nutrients to make sure they get everything they need throughout the day.
- It gives your child's physical and emotional well-being a boost, especially if you are serving healthy and tasty snacks they'll enjoy eating.
- It helps them remain energized throughout the day.
- It allows them to perform better at school.

Naturally, your child can only get all of these benefits from snacking if they snack wisely and healthily.

SNACKING WISELY VS. SNACKING MINDLESSLY

As a parent, you already know that what your child eats is very important for their growth and development. But this doesn't just apply to their regular meals. You should also teach your child to be mindful of what they snack on, to help them develop the proper habits as they grow up. Unfortunately, many adults these days who tend to snack mindlessly learned these habits as children. Allowing your child to consume their meals and snacks regularly will help maintain the health of their digestive system. When your child follows an irregular eating schedule, they might experience indigestion, gas, and other digestive issues. So, if you want your child to feel comfortable, happy, and energized throughout the day, don't forget their snacks!

When it comes to snacking, there is a proper and improper way to do it. For instance, reaching for a bag of chips every hour and eating everything in the bag is not a proper way to enjoy a snack—and it's not an ideal snack, either. To help your child learn to snack wisely instead of mindlessly, you have to guide them. Here are some tips for doing this:

Come up with a schedule and a plan for your child's meals and snacks

Meal planning is a wonderful practice that will allow you to keep track of your child's meals and help them learn healthy eating habits. From breakfast to dinner and everything in between, come up with a plan for what you will serve your child. It would also be helpful to come up with a schedule for your child's meal and snack times. While you don't have to force your child to follow this schedule strictly, having the schedule helps remind you when it's time for your child to eat.

Make sure your child is well-hydrated throughout the day

If you notice that your child is always asking for a snack even after they have just eaten, they might just be thirsty or dehydrated. Make sure that your child drinks enough water throughout the day to cleanse their body and keep them healthy and strong.

Encourage your child to treat snack time as a proper meal

One of the most common reasons why people—both adults and children—snack mindlessly is that they are distracted while eating. If your child is doing something else while eating, like watching TV or playing with their friends, they won't notice what they are eating or how much they have eaten. Soon, your child will either leave their snack half-eaten or they will have eaten more than they were supposed to. But if you encourage your child to sit down and eat their snacks the same way as their meals, they will learn how to be more mindful.

Prepare healthy and satisfying snacks for your child

If you want to make sure that your child is eating healthy snacks, you have to prepare these for them, especially at the beginning. Right now, your child may be used to store-bought snacks that, unfortunately, are filled with unhealthy ingredients. It's time to change your child's habits by preparing healthy snacks for them to enjoy every time they feel hungry.

Encourage your child to opt for healthier snack options

Healthy snacks will make your child feel fuller, more satisfied, and become healthier. Another way to help your child learn how to make healthier food choices is by encouraging them to eat healthy foods, especially while they are still young. Some examples of healthy snack options are wholegrains like low-sodium tortilla chips or pretzels, gluten-free granola, peanut butter on apple slices, and nuts. When it comes to snacks, the sky's the limit!

Although you ultimately want your child to learn how to eat healthily even during snack time, you need to guide them, especially as they transition to the gluten-free diet. Remember that snacking is an important part of your child's diet and as a parent, you should plan your child's snacks and have these ready at the right times. As you serve healthy snacks, explain these to your child to help them understand the importance of snacking wisely.

With all of these things in mind, here are some amazingly easy recipes that your child will look forward to whenever snack time rolls around.

CLASSIC CORN DOGS

Kids love corn dogs, and even if your child transitions to the gluten-free diet, they can still enjoy this fun treat in a different way. Here's a recipe for you to whip up a classic snack with a twist that your child will surely appreciate, while making you feel nostalgic.

Time: 25 minutes

Serving Size: 16 corn dogs

Prep Time: 5 minutes

Cook Time: 20 minutes

Ingredients:

- ½ tsp olive oil
- ½ tsp salt
- ½ tsp xanthan gum
- ½ tbsp potato starch flour
- 1 tbsp baking powder
- ¼ cup of chives (finely chopped)
- ¼ cup of onion (sliced)
- ¼ cup of sugar
- ½ cup of almond meal
- ½ cup of olive oil
- ⅔ cup of milk
- ¾ cup of gluten-free flour
- 1 cup of cornmeal
- 1 ½ cups of sausage (gluten-free, diced)
- 3 large eggs
- Cooking spray

Directions:

1. Preheat your oven to 350 F and use cooking spray to grease a muffin pan.
2. In a skillet, add ½ teaspoon of olive oil and the

onions, then cook over medium heat until caramelized.
3. Once done, take the skillet off the stove and set aside.
4. In a bowl, combine all of the dry ingredients except the sausage and chives.
5. In a separate bowl, add the eggs, milk, and olive oil. Mix until well combined.
6. Pour the mixture into the bowl with the dry ingredients and gently stir together. You should have a wet batter.
7. Leave the batter to sit and thicken for about 2 minutes before stirring in the chives, sausages, and caramelized onions.
8. Pour the batter evenly into the muffin pan.
9. Place the muffin pan in the oven and bake the corn dogs for about 20 minutes. Around 15 minutes into the cooking time, check to see if the corn dogs have golden brown bottoms but light-colored tops. Keep checking until you're sure that the corn dogs are completely cooked through.
10. Take the muffin pan out of the oven and allow the corn dogs to cool before serving.

GUILT-FREE CHOCOLATE PUDDING

If your child is asking you for something sweet, you can serve this super easy snack. It's healthy, it doesn't require any cooking, and it will definitely satisfy any sweet tooth. You should prepare this beforehand since it requires at least an hour of chilling time. And when snack time comes along, all you have to do is serve it.

Time: 6 minutes (plus chilling time)

Serving Size: 2 servings

Prep Time: 6 minutes

Cook Time: no cooking time

Ingredients:

- 1 large banana (very ripe)
- ½ cup of Greek yogurt (plain)
- 2 tbsp cocoa powder (unsweetened)

- 1 tbsp peanut butter (optional, to taste, you can also use other types of nut butter)

Directions:

1. In a food processor, add all of the ingredients, including the peanut butter if using. Blend everything until you get a smooth texture.
2. Pour the pudding into serving bowls and cover with cling wrap.
3. Place the bowls in the refrigerator and allow the pudding to chill for a minimum of 1 hour.
4. Serve chilled. You may top the pudding with banana slices, too.

SWEET POTATO SHOESTRING FRIES

One taste of these crunchy shoestring fries and your child will be hooked! The good news is, this dish is a healthy snack that doesn't come with the empty calories you'll find in processed potato chips. You can even make this recipe more interesting by using your own mix of seasonings and spices to create a different flavor each time you serve it.

Time: 40 minutes

Serving Size: 2 servings

Prep Time: 10 minutes

Cook Time: 30 minutes

Ingredients:

- 1 tbsp olive oil (you can also use coconut oil)
- 1 sweet potato (peeled)
- Cooking spray
- Salt

Directions:

1. Preheat your oven to 375 F and use cooking spray to grease a cookie sheet.
2. Cut the sweet potato into julienne strips.
3. In a bowl, add the sweet potato strings and olive oil toss until evenly coated.
4. Transfer the shoestring fries to the cookie sheet and spread them out evenly in a single layer.
5. Place the cookie sheet in the oven and bake the fries for about 30 minutes. Every 10 minutes, stir the fries around to ensure they cook evenly.
6. Once cooked, take the cookie sheet out of the oven.
7. Sprinkle the fries with salt and toss to coat. Remove any that have been over-baked.

8. Allow the fries to cool to room temperature before serving.

MINI CANDY CORN MUFFINS

These fun muffins are a great snack and a fun Halloween treat, too! They look fantastic and taste even better. You can make these mini muffins or you can make them into regular-sized muffins for parties. Just adjust the cooking times as needed.

Time: 35 minutes

Serving Size: 30 mini muffins

Prep Time: 22 minutes

Cook Time: 13 minutes

Ingredients for the mini muffins:

- ¾ tsp cinnamon (ground)
- 2 tsp vanilla extract
- ¼ cup of olive oil (you can also use grapeseed oil)
- 1 cup of water (cold)
- 1 box of muffin mix (gluten-free, store-bought, or you can make your own muffin batter from scratch)
- Cooking spray

Ingredients for the frosting:

- 1 tsp vanilla extract
- 1 tbsp milk (preferably dairy-free)
- ⅓ cup of chocolate chips
- ½ cup of buttery spread (preferably dairy-free)
- 2 cups of confectioners' sugar
- Food coloring (yellow and red)

Directions:

1. Preheat your oven to 350 F and use cooking spray to grease a mini muffin tin.
2. In a bowl, mix together all of the muffin ingredients. Compare this list of ingredients with the recommended ingredients in the muffin mix you have bought and adjust as needed.
3. Pour the batter into the muffin tin. Fill each of the cups about halfway.
4. Place the muffin tin in the oven and bake the muffins for 10 to 13 minutes. Again, check the box of the muffin mix you bought and adjust the cooking time as needed.
5. Take the muffin tin out of the oven and allow the muffins to cool for about 10 minutes before

transferring them to a wire rack to cool down completely.

6. In a bowl, add the buttery spread and use a hand mixer to beat on high for about 1 minute.
7. Add 1 ½ cups of the sugar and continue beating for about 2 minutes more until you get a fluffy, light, and smooth texture.
8. Add the rest of the sugar, vanilla extract, and milk, then continue beating for 1 minute more until you get a creamy and smooth mixture.
9. Add the chocolate chips and fold them in gently.
10. Divide the frosting into 3 equal portions.
11. Mix yellow food coloring into the first portion to create the yellow frosting.
12. Mix yellow and red food coloring into the second portion to create the orange frosting. The third portion will remain white.
13. Transfer all of the frosting portions into piping bags and chill in the refrigerator for at least 15 minutes.
14. When you're ready to frost the muffins, take the piping bags out of the refrigerator.
15. Start with the orange frosting, then add the yellow frosting, and finish with the white frosting at the top.
16. Serve with a smile!

QUINOA VEGGIE BITES

This is a healthy and savory snack that only requires four ingredients to put together. You can even customize the recipe by using any frozen or leftover vegetables you have. This is an awesome snack option as you can sneak protein, veggies, and quinoa into your child's diet in a crunchy and tasty way.

Time: 30 minutes

Serving Size: 6 servings

Prep Time: 10 minutes

Cook Time: 20 minutes

Ingredients:

- ½ tsp kosher salt
- 1 cup of cheddar cheese (shredded)
- 1 cup of quinoa (cooked, cooled)
- 1 cup of vegetables of your choice (steamed, boiled or roasted, chopped)
- 1 egg
- Cooking spray

Directions:

1. Preheat your oven to 350 F and use cooking spray to grease a mini muffin tin.
2. In a bowl, add all of the ingredients then mix thoroughly until well-combined.
3. Spoon the mixture into the muffin tin and press down with the back of the spoon to make the veggie bites firm.
4. Place the muffin tin in the oven and bake the veggie bites for about 15 to 20 minutes until crispy and golden brown.
5. Take the muffin tin out of the oven and allow the veggie bites to cool down before serving.

SWEET AND HEALTHY PARFAITS

Have you ever tried giving your child a parfait? This delicious dish looks amazingly fancy, but it's very easy to make. This recipe makes a sweet parfait with healthy ingredients that fits right into the gluten-free diet.

Time: 5 minutes

Serving Size: 4 servings

Prep Time: 5 minutes

Cook Time: no cooking time

Ingredients:

- 2 tsp honey
- 1 cup of granola (gluten-free)
- 1 ¼ cups of yogurt (vanilla flavor, you can also use plain or Greek yogurt)
- 1 ½ cups of mixed berries (raspberries, blueberries, and strawberries)

Directions:

1. In each of the parfait glasses, create layers of granola, yogurt, and mixed berries by spooning the ingredients one layer at a time until you reach the top.
2. The top should be a layer of yogurt, then garnish this with a sprinkle of granola or a fresh berry.
3. You can serve the parfaits right away or chill them in the refrigerator for a while before serving.

HEALTHY HOMEMADE CHIPS

For children, potato chips are the ultimate snack. You can make these healthy potato chips in your kitchen and serve them to your child without worrying about unhealthy additives. These chips are delicious, crispy, and super easy to make. You can also experiment with different seasonings to make things more interesting for your child.

Time: 12 minutes

Serving Size: 2 servings

Prep Time: 5 minutes

Cook Time: 7 minutes

Ingredients:

- 1 large potato (preferably a russet potato, peeled)
- Salt (preferably ultra-fine)

Directions:

1. Slice the potato thinly. You can use a food processor or a mandolin for this.
2. Line a microwave-safe plate with parchment paper.

3. Place the potato slices on the plate in one layer and sprinkle with salt.
4. Place the plate in the microwave and cook on high for about 3 to 7 minutes. The cooking time depends on your microwave and how thick your potato slices are. You'll know the chips are done when they're slightly golden and very crispy.
5. Take the plate out of the oven (be careful, it will be super hot) and transfer the potato chips to a bowl. If needed, cook the potato chips in batches.
6. Allow the potato chips to cool down before serving.

CRISPY GRANOLA BARS

These no-bake bars are crispy, crunchy, and they store well, too. This means you can whip up a batch of these snack bars and have them ready whenever your child is craving something sweet. You can even serve these for breakfast on your busiest mornings.

Time: 10 minutes

Serving Size: 12 bars

Prep Time: 10 minutes

Cook Time: no cooking time

Ingredients:

- ½ tsp kosher salt
- 1 tsp vanilla extract
- 4 tbsp coconut oil
- ½ cup of coconut chips (unsweetened)
- ½ cup of honey
- ½ cup of oat flour
- 1 cup of light brown sugar (you can also use coconut palm sugar)
- 2 cups of rice cereal (gluten-free)
- 2 cups of rolled oats

Directions:

1. Use parchment paper to line a baking dish. Crisscross the sheets of parchment paper, ensuring that the sheets overhang all sides of the baking dish. After preparing the dish, set it aside.
2. In a saucepan, add the coconut oil, sugar, and salt over medium heat.
3. Cook until the ingredients liquefy, stirring occasionally. Once liquefied, allow to simmer for about 45 seconds without stirring.
4. Take the saucepan off of the heat and add the vanilla extract and honey.

5. Stir the mixture constantly until you no longer see bubbles.
6. Allow it to cool down until you can touch it with your fingers.
7. In a bowl, add all of the dry ingredients and mix well.
8. Use your fingers to make a well in the middle of the dry ingredients.
9. Pour the sugar mixture into the well then mix quickly and thoroughly until the dry ingredients have been completely absorbed.
10. Transfer the mixture into the baking dish and spread it out evenly.
11. You can allow the mixture to cool at room temperature or you can place the baking dish in the refrigerator.
12. Once cooled, pull the overhanging parchment paper up to remove the uncut bars from the baking dish.
13. Cut the bars into rectangles and wrap each one with parchment paper.
14. Serve at snack time!

CAULIFLOWER TOTS

Just like the veggie bites, these cauliflower tots are crispy, healthy, and totally kid-friendly. You can serve these tots at parties, as a side dish, and as a healthy snack for your child at home or at school. Since they're made of veggies, these tots will add more nutrients to your child's diet.

Time: 40 minutes

Serving Size: 4 servings

Prep Time: 15 minutes

Cook Time: 25 minutes

Ingredients:

- ½ tsp mustard (ground)
- 1 tsp kosher salt
- ¼ cup of cornmeal (you can also use ground oats)
- 1 cup of sharp cheddar cheese (shredded)
- 3 cups cauliflower (shredded)
- 1 egg
- Black pepper
- Cooking spray

Directions:

1. Preheat your oven to 400 F and use cooking spray to grease a mini muffin tin.
2. Place the cauliflower in a cheesecloth and wring it out to remove the excess water.
3. In a bowl, mix together all of the ingredients.
4. Spoon the mixture into the muffin tin and use the back of the spoon to press down. This will make your tots firm.
5. Place the muffin tin in the oven and bake the tots for about 20 to 25 minutes.
6. Take the muffin tin out of the oven and allow the tots to cool before transferring them to a bowl or plate.
7. Serve while warm and crispy.

GRAHAM CRACKERS

This recipe is so versatile, as you can use different kinds of cookie cutters to make cookies of different shapes. It's a fun way to serve healthy gluten-free cookies to your child during snack time. They also store well, too, so you can bake these in advance.

Time: 20 minutes

Serving Size: depends on the size and shape of your cookie cutters

Prep Time: 10 minutes

Cook Time: 10 minutes

Ingredients:

- ½ tsp baking soda
- ½ tsp cinnamon
- ½ tsp vanilla extract
- 2 tsp egg replacer
- 1 tbsp molasses
- 2 tbsp palm shortening (melted)
- 3 tbsp ice water
- 1 cup of all-purpose flour (gluten-free)
- Sugar (powdered, for dusting)

Directions:

1. In a bowl, mix together all of the dry ingredients except the sugar.
2. In a microwave-safe bowl, add the shortening and melt it in the microwave.
3. Add the hot shortening to the dry ingredient mixture, along with the molasses and the egg replacer.
4. Mix well until you get a crumbly and dry dough.

5. Add the ice water one tablespoon at a time until a stickier dough forms.
6. Once you have formed the dough, knead it with your hands.
7. Place the dough on a sheet of parchment paper and place another sheet on top.
8. Roll the dough out with a rolling pin until it's about ⅛-inch thick.
9. Use cookie cutters to cut out shapes.
10. Place the cookies on a cookie sheet lined with parchment paper.
11. Place the cookie sheet in the oven preheated to 350 F and bake for about 8 to 10 minutes.
12. Take the baking sheet out of the oven and dust the cookies with sugar.
13. Allow the cookies to cool down before serving.

BAKED MOZZARELLA STICKS

This snack is gooey, cheesy, and oh-so-delicious. It's another savory snack recipe to add to your gluten-free arsenal and it's sure to be very popular with your whole family. Pair them with a bowl of gluten-free marinara sauce for dipping and watch these baked mozzarella sticks disappear as your child gobbles them up!

Time: 56 minutes

Serving Size: 24 mozzarella sticks

Prep Time: 50 minutes

Cook Time: 6 minutes

Ingredients:

- 2 tbsp flour (gluten-free)
- 2 tbsp Parmesan cheese (grated)
- 6 tbsp almond flour (you can also use gluten-free bread crumbs)
- 1 egg
- 12 mozzarella sticks
- Cooking spray

Directions:

1. Cut each of the mozzarella sticks lengthwise so that you have 24 sticks.
2. Place the mozzarella sticks on a cookie sheet lined with parchment paper and put the sheet in the refrigerator for about 30 minutes.
3. In one bowl, add the flour. In a second bowl, add the egg and beat it. In a third bowl, add the parmesan cheese and almond flour, then mix well.

4. Take the chilled mozzarella sticks out of the refrigerator.
5. Coat each of the mozzarella sticks with flour, egg, and the Parmesan cheese mixture, then place back on the cookie sheet.
6. Place the cookie sheet back in the refrigerator and chill the mozzarella sticks for at least 15 minutes.
7. Preheat your oven to 400 F, line another cookie sheet with foil, and grease it with cooking spray.
8. Take the mozzarella sticks out of the refrigerator and place them on the greased cookie sheet.
9. Place the cookie sheet in the oven and bake for about 3 minutes.
10. Flip each of the mozzarella sticks over and continue baking for 3 minutes more.
11. Take the cookie sheet out of the oven and allow the mozzarella sticks to cool down. Serve with marinara sauce for dipping.

PUMPKIN BROWNIE BARS

Pumpkin in brownies? Your child might raise their eyebrows at this combination, but one bite of these brownies will change their mind. This yummy recipe has a lovely sweetness along with the unique flavor from the pumpkin. Try it out and taste it for yourself.

Time: 1 hour and 5 minutes

Serving Size: 16 large brownies

Prep Time: 10 minutes

Cook Time: 55 minutes

Ingredients for the brownie mix:

- 2 tbsp olive oil (you can also use grapeseed oil)
- ¾ cup of water (cold)
- 1 box of brownie mix (gluten-free)

Ingredients for the pumpkin mix:

- ¼ tsp cloves (ground)
- ¼ tsp ginger (ground)
- ¼ tsp nutmeg (ground)
- ½ tsp vanilla extract
- 1 tsp cinnamon (ground)
- ¼ cup of all-purpose flour (gluten-free)

- ¼ cup of maple syrup
- 1 ¼ cup of pumpkin (cooked, mashed)
- Salt

Ingredients for the topping:

- 2 tsp olive oil (you can also use grapeseed oil)
- ¼ cup of chocolate chips

Directions:

1. Preheat your oven to 375 F and use parchment paper to line a baking pan.
2. In a bowl, combine all of the brownie mix ingredients and mix well. Check the box of the brownie mix you bought and adjust the ingredients accordingly.
3. Pour the brownie mix into the baking pan and spread evenly.
4. Place the baking pan in the oven and bake the brownies for about 15 minutes.
5. In a separate bowl, add all of the pumpkin mix ingredients and mix well.
6. After the brownies have baked for 15 minutes, take the baking pan out of the oven and pour the pumpkin mix in.

7. Swirl the pumpkin mix into the brownie batter.
8. Place the baking pan back into the oven and continue cooking the brownies for about 35 to 40 minutes more.
9. In a microwave-safe bowl, add the oil and chocolate chips. Place the bowl in the microwave to melt the chocolate chips for about 15 seconds on high.
10. Mix the ingredients together. If the chocolate chips aren't completely melted, continue microwaving for 10 seconds more.
11. Take the baking pan out of the oven and drizzle the top with the melted chocolate.
12. Allow the brownies to cool completely before cutting into bars and serving as a snack.

PILLOW-SOFT MINI PRETZELS

These hot, chewy pretzels are amazingly delicious. You can serve them with cheese, peanut butter, or even on their own. This is a simple recipe that uses simple ingredients, but the result you will come up with is incredible!

Time: 1 hour and 35 minutes

Serving Size: 8 servings

Prep Time: 1 hour and 25 minutes

Cook Time: 10 minutes

Ingredients for the baking soda mix:

- ⅛ tsp sea salt
- 1 ½ tbsp baking soda
- 10 cups of water

Ingredients for the pretzels:

- 1 tsp baking powder
- 1 tsp salt
- 1 tbsp active dry yeast
- 1 tbsp olive oil (more for coating)
- 1 tbsp sugar
- 1 cup of water
- 3 ½ cups of flour (gluten-free)

Directions:

1. In a bowl, combine baking soda powder, yeast, and water.
2. Allow the mixture to sit for a couple of minutes until bubbles start to form.
3. In a bowl, add the baking powder, salt, and flour, then use a hand mixer to combine.

4. Add the yeast mixture and the oil, then continue mixing until you form a dough.
5. Knead the dough for another 1 to 2 minutes and form into a ball.
6. Lightly brush the surface of the dough with oil, cover with cling wrap, and leave for about 1 hour to rise at room temperature.
7. Preheat your oven to 425 F and use parchment paper to line a baking sheet.
8. In a saucepan, add the baking soda and 10 cups of water, then bring to a rolling boil over medium heat.
9. Transfer the dough onto a lightly oiled surface and divide it into 5 pieces.
10. Roll each piece out into a long rope, then slice each rope into 1-inch strips.
11. Place strips of the dough into a slotted spoon and lower the slotted spoon into the saucepan of boiling water.
12. Boil the mini pretzels for about 30 seconds while swirling the slotted spoon around to flip them.
13. Lift the slotted spoon, drain the water, and transfer the mini pretzels to the baking sheet.
14. Repeat the boiling steps until you have boiled all of the mini pretzel bites.

15. Brush the surface of each mini pretzel with olive oil then sprinkle with a bit of salt.
16. Place the baking sheet in the oven and bake the mini pretzels for about 10 to 12 minutes until they are golden brown.
17. Take the baking sheet out of the oven and allow the mini pretzels to cool slightly.
18. Serve the mini pretzel bites while still warm.

FRUIT PLATTER WITH SWEET HUMMUS DIP

Serving a fruit platter as a snack will surely delight your kids, thanks to all of the vibrant colors. Pair the fresh fruits with sweet and healthy hummus for a filling and fun treat. The hummus in this recipe is chock-full of fiber and protein, which makes it an ideal addition to your child's diet.

Time: 10 minutes

Serving Size: 14 servings

Prep Time: 10 minutes

Cook Time: no cooking time

Ingredients:

- ¼ tsp salt
- 1 tsp pumpkin pie spice
- 1 tsp vanilla extract
- 3 tbsp honey (you can also use maple or agave syrup)
- ½ cup of mini chocolate chips (more for topping)
- ½ cup of pumpkin purée
- 1 ¾ cups of chickpeas (canned, rinsed, drained, dried, liquid reserved)
- Fruit slices of your choice (for dipping)

Directions:

1. In a food processor, add the pumpkin pie spice, vanilla extract, honey, pumpkin purée, chickpeas, and salt.
2. Process the ingredients until you get a smooth texture. If needed, add some of the chickpea liquid to get the texture you want.
3. Pour the hummus into a bowl and fold in the chocolate chips. Sprinkle with more chocolate chips if desired.
4. Place the bowl of hummus in the middle of a serving plate and arrange the sliced fruits around it before serving.

TASTY PIZZA BITES

These pizza bites are so quick, yummy, and have no crusts—which is great, because most kids don't like crusts anyway. As with any other pizza recipe, you can mix and match the toppings for these savory little bites. You can even ask your child to help you top the pizza bites with their favorite ingredients!

Time: 50 minutes

Serving Size: 12 servings

Prep Time: 10 minutes

Cook Time: 40 minutes

Ingredients:

- ½ cup of mozzarella cheese (shredded)
- ½ cup of pineapple chunks (canned, drained)
- ½ cup of pizza sauce (store-bought or homemade)
- 24 slices of Canadian bacon (thick-cut)
- Cooking spray
- Other toppings of your choice

Directions:

1. Preheat your oven to 350 F and use cooking spray to grease a muffin tin.
2. Line each of the muffin cups with 3 slices of Canadian bacon and press down firmly.
3. Spoon about 1 tablespoon of sauce over the slices of bacon.
4. Top with shredded mozzarella, pineapple chunks, and any other toppings you desire.
5. Place the muffin tin in the oven and bake the pizza bites for about 25 minutes, until the cheese starts bubbling.
6. Take the muffin tin out of the oven and allow the pizza bites to cool down before serving.

STICKY CHIA PUDDING

This snack is sticky, sweet, creamy, and packed with healthy ingredients. You can serve it as a filling snack or a sweet breakfast. It even comes with sticky maple pecans that add some crunch and flavor to the whole dish. Yum!

Time: 15 minutes

Serving Size: 4 servings

Prep Time: 10 minutes

Cook Time: 5 minutes

Ingredients for the pudding:

- 1 tsp cinnamon (ground)
- 1 tsp vanilla extract
- 1 tbsp brown sugar
- 2 tbsp agave nectar
- ½ cup of chia seeds
- 2 cups of cashew milk (unsweetened)

Ingredients for the pecans:

- 2 tbsp agave nectar
- 2 tbsp maple syrup
- ¾ cup of pecans (chopped)
- Salt

Directions:

1. In a bowl, combine all of the pudding ingredients and mix well.

2. Cover the bowl with cling wrap and leave it in the refrigerator overnight.
3. In a saucepan, mix together the agave nectar, maple syrup, and a pinch of salt, and bring to a boil.
4. Once boiling, take the saucepan off the heat and add the pecans.
5. Mix well to coat the pecans then allow to sit for about 5 minutes.
6. Take the pudding out of the refrigerator and spoon into serving bowls. Top each bowl with sticky pecans and serve.

PIZZA WITH ORANGE SAUCE

Kids just love pizza, don't they? Here's one pizza recipe that has a unique look and an equally unique taste. You can even call it rainbow pizza to make it more fun for your child to eat. This pizza is also perfect for the fall season, as its sauce is mainly made of pumpkin.

Time: 50 minutes

Serving Size: 2 medium-sized pizzas

Prep Time: 15 minutes

Cook Time: 35 minutes

Ingredients for the pizza:

- 1 tsp oregano (dried)
- ½ cup of bacon (chopped)
- ½ cup of red onion (chopped)
- 1 ¼ cup of water (cold)
- 1 ½ cup of broccoli (chopped)
- 1 box of pizza crust mix (store-bought, but you can also make your own or opt for frozen gluten-free pizza crust)
- Black pepper
- Olive oil (for brushing)
- Salt

Ingredients for the sauce:

- 1 tbsp maple syrup
- 2 tbsp of olive oil
- 3 cups of butternut squash (cut into cubes)
- 3 cloves of garlic (skin removed)
- Black pepper
- Cooking spray
- Sea salt

Directions:

1. Preheat your oven to 400 F and use cooking spray to grease 2 baking sheets.
2. Place the butternut squash and garlic on the first baking sheet.
3. Season with 1 tablespoon of olive oil, salt, and pepper, then toss lightly to coat.
4. Place the baking sheet in the oven and roast the veggies for about 15 to 20 minutes.
5. After roasting, take the baking sheet out of the oven and transfer the veggies into a blender.
6. Add the maple syrup and the rest of the olive oil then blend until you get a smooth, spreadable consistency. Set aside.
7. In a bowl, add the pizza crust mix and water. Add the water gradually while mixing until you form a dough.
8. Knead the dough for about 1 to 2 minutes then divide into 2 portions.
9. Roll the dough portions into balls.
10. Place the dough balls on a lightly floured surface and roll them out to your desired crust thickness.
11. Place the pizza crusts on the second baking sheet, brush each pizza crust with olive oil, and sprinkle with salt, pepper, and dried oregano.
12. Use a fork to poke holes all over the crusts.

13. Place the baking sheet in the oven and bake the pizza crusts for about 8 to 10 minutes.
14. Take the baking sheet out of the oven and top the pizza crusts with broccoli, bacon, and red onion.
15. Place the baking sheet back into the oven and bake for 10 to 12 more minutes.
16. Take the baking sheet out of the oven and allow the pizzas to cool down for a while before slicing and serving.

BAGEL CHIPS WITH RAISINS AND CINNAMON

This yummy snack has the perfect blend of salty and sweet flavors. You can serve them at home or give them to your child as a snack for school. These bagel chips are very easy to make and they have a satisfying crunch that your child will surely love.

Time: 52 minutes

Serving Size: 2 servings

Prep Time: 15 minutes

Cook Time: 37 minutes

Ingredients:

- ¼ tsp salt
- ½ tsp allspice
- ¾ tsp cinnamon
- 2 tbsp coconut sugar
- 4 tbsp olive oil
- 2 cinnamon raisin bagels (gluten-free)

Directions:

1. Preheat your oven to 250°F and use parchment paper to line a cookie sheet.
2. In a bowl, combine the cinnamon, allspice, coconut sugar, and salt. Mix well then set aside.
3. Slice the bagels horizontally into 6 thin slices each.
4. Lay each slice on the cookie sheet.
5. Brush each of the bagels with olive oil and sprinkle with the seasoning mixture.
6. Place the cookie sheet in the oven and bake the bagel chips for about 22 minutes.
7. Take the cookie sheet out of the oven and flip the bagel chips over. Brush each one with olive oil and sprinkle with the seasoning mixture, then place the cookie sheet back in the oven and bake for 15 minutes more.
8. Take the cookie sheet out of the oven and allow the bagel chips to cool down before serving.

CHEESY BAKED CRISPS

Crispy bites of cheddar and Parmesan cheese? Doesn't that sound divine? This is a super fast and easy recipe, which means that you can have a snack ready for your child in a flash. The best part is, you only need three ingredients to make it!

Time: 12 minutes

Serving Size: 4 servings

Prep Time: 5 minutes

Cook Time: 7 minutes

Ingredients:

- ¾ cup of cheddar cheese (shredded)
- ¾ cup of Parmesan cheese (shredded)
- 1 tsp Italian seasoning (optional)

Directions:

1. Preheat your oven to 400 F and use parchment paper to line a baking sheet.
2. In a bowl, combine the cheddar cheese, Parmesan cheese, and Italian seasoning, if desired.

3. Use a spoon to transfer heaps of the cheese mixture to the baking sheet. Make sure there is enough space between each heap as the crisps tend to spread out while baking.
4. Place the baking sheet in the oven and bake the cheese crisps for about 6 to 8 minutes.
5. Take the baking sheet out of the oven and allow the cheese crisps to cool down before serving them as a snack.

FROZEN PROTEIN BARS

Protein bars are healthy, filling, and they taste delicious, too. This recipe is nutty, cinnamon-y, and has the right amount of sweetness to satisfy your child's sweet tooth. With these protein bars, you will feel great about your child's snack because you know that they contain healthy ingredients that fit right into your child's diet.

Time: 10 minutes

Serving Size: 15 bars

Prep Time: 10 minutes

Cook Time: no cooking time

Ingredients:

- 1 tsp vanilla extract
- 1 tsp cinnamon
- ½ cup of almond butter
- ½ cup of almonds (raw)
- ½ cup of cashews (raw)
- ½ cup of maple syrup
- 1 ½ cups of puffed rice (gluten-free)
- Olive oil (for coating)

Directions:

1. In a food processor, process the almonds and cashews until you get a coarse powder.
2. In a saucepan, add the almond butter and maple syrup over low heat. Heat until the ingredients melt together.
3. Once melted and combined, take the saucepan off the heat, add the cinnamon and vanilla extract, then mix until well combined.
4. In a bowl, combine the ground nuts with the heated liquid and mix well.
5. Add the puffed rice and mix until all ingredients are well combined.
6. Lightly grease a baking dish with olive oil then transfer the mixture into it.

7. Use a spatula to spread the mixture out and flatten it.
8. Place the baking dish in your freezer for at least 30 minutes.
9. Once set, take the baking dish out of the freezer and slice the protein bars.
10. Serve and enjoy!

6

LUNCH IDEAS THAT WILL MAKE YOUR CHILD'S FRIENDS JEALOUS

Packing a lunch box for your child can already feel quite tedious—and it feels even more daunting if your child needs to follow certain dietary restrictions. As with breakfast and snacks, you don't have to fret, because there are so many lunch ideas you can prepare for your child on a gluten-free diet. Lunchtime is one of your child's main meals and if they go to school, they will typically have their lunch there. If you want your child to stick with their special diet, you must prepare amazing school lunches for them. To encourage your child, prepare dishes that they will enjoy eating—lunch boxes that will make their friends jealous!

HAVING LUNCH AT SCHOOL

It's much easier to encourage your child to follow a gluten-free diet at home. You can control your child's environment, guide them, and encourage them each time they eat their meals or snacks. But when your child goes to school, all you can do is trust them to make the right decisions for themselves.

Whenever children eat their lunch at school, they are strongly influenced by their peers. If your child sees that their classmates are eating unhealthy foods, there is a very high likelihood that they will ask you to pack the same types of food in their lunchbox, too. However, if your child must follow a gluten-free diet because they suffer from celiac disease, then you can't give in to such requests. As a parent, you must understand the power of peer pressure and social influences. All children will experience these things at one point or another. And if your child is struggling with such issues, they might not want to eat the lunchboxes you prepare for them.

These days, children have to deal with things like judgments, cliques, and other negative experiences that make school very challenging. If these things interfere with your child's transition to a gluten-free diet, you need to do something about it. Try approaching your child's diet in a positive way.

Focus on encouragement instead of trying to force your child to adjust to their diet without feeling isolated from their peers. Here are some tips to help you out:

Introduce your child to different types of food

As you help your child transition to a gluten-free diet, introduce them to different types of food. These days, there are gluten-free alternatives to all kinds of foods. Instead of making huge changes to your child's diet, help them adapt gradually. Every week, introduce a new type of food to your child until they get used to gluten-free foods.

Help your child enjoy lunchtime at school

If your child is feeling shy or embarrassed about their lunches because their meals are different from their classmates', you can turn things around by making your child's lunch box more interesting than those of their friends. When your child sees that other children are interested in their lunch, they will surely feel more confident. If you can create meals that taste great and look amazing, you can make lunchtime more enjoyable for your child, no matter how different their food is from their peers'.

Allow your child to help you create gluten-free masterpieces

In line with the previous point, another thing you can do to help your child enjoy and appreciate their meals more is by inviting them to help you prepare meals. When children are given the chance to prepare and "cook" their own meals, they will feel more interested in eating those meals, too. Once or twice a week, choose simple recipes and invite your child to help you prepare their lunchbox for school. You can also do this fun tip for your child's breakfast, dinner, and snacks.

Remind your child to ask before sharing

In school, one thing you cannot control is when your child shares their food with others. If it's your child who shares their food with their friends, that's okay. But if your child's friends share their food—and it contains gluten—this will pose a risk to your child. The best thing you can do is to remind your child to ask their friends what their food is before sharing. It's better to educate your child as early as possible to help them learn how to follow their special diet safely. If your child is a bit younger, you can ask their teacher for help with this.

Plan ahead for parties and events

While your child is in school, there may be days when they will have parties and other social events that involve food. This is okay, as long as you plan ahead. If your child is on a gluten-free diet, talk to their teacher and ask if they can inform you ahead of time of any upcoming events. That way, you can plan to contribute food to the party so that your child will have something to eat. Either that or you can plan a special lunchbox for your child for the event so they won't feel left out.

Whenever you have to bring up the subject of food with your child, try to be as positive and encouraging as possible. You want to show your child love and support so that they feel better about the diet they have to follow. And one of the best ways you can do this is by learning how to make amazing dishes that your child will enjoy.

LUNCH IS AN IMPORTANT MEAL, TOO

While breakfast will provide your child with the energy they need for the whole morning, that isn't enough. Your child needs to eat regular meals throughout the day to remain healthy, strong, and energized. One such meal is lunch, and this is one of the most important meals they will eat each day. During weekends, you can eat the same meals together as a family. But when your child is at school, you have to prepare yummy, healthy meals for them to eat along with their friends.

If you can make interesting meals for your child, this can help them feel more confident. As soon as your child opens their lunch box, they can show off meals that look amazing and taste amazing, too. This will allow your child to interact happily with their friends during their lunch break, and perhaps even help their friends understand why your child's meals differ from their own. This understanding will come with acceptance, which will make your child feel better about their diet. In other words, if you can prepare appetizing lunch boxes for your child, you will set them up for success. Here are some quick, easy, and scrumptious gluten-free lunch recipes that will surely make your child the talk of the town .. in a good way!

FRESH LETTUCE WRAPS

These lettuce wraps are crunchy, refreshing, and oh-so-yummy. They come with a creamy dipping sauce and a filling that's mildly spicy. As you whip up this dish for your child, you can also share it with the rest of your family for lunch.

Time: 20 minutes

Serving Size: 10 servings

Prep Time: 10 servings

Cook Time: 10 servings

Ingredients for the chicken wraps:

- 2 tbsp hoisin sauce
- 2 tbsp sesame oil
- 2 tbsp soy sauce (you can also use tamari)
- 1 cup of baby carrots (chopped using a food processor)
- 2 lbs of ground chicken
- 1 head of lettuce (iceberg or romaine)
- 2 limes (juiced)
- 3 cloves of garlic (chopped)
- 1 tbsp sriracha sauce (optional)

Ingredients for the sauce:

- 1 tsp hoisin sauce
- 1 tsp lime juice
- 2 tbsp peanut butter
- 2 tbsp rice vinegar
- 2 tbsp tamari
- 3 tbsp water (warm)

Directions:

1. Wash the lettuce and separate the leaves. You will use the leaves for wrapping.
2. In a skillet, warm the sesame oil and brown the chicken over medium heat.
3. Cook the ground chicken until completely cooked through.
4. Add the carrots and garlic then continue cooking for about 2 to 3 minutes more.
5. Add the soy sauce, hoisin sauce, and sriracha sauce, if using, then mix well as you continue cooking for about 2 to 3 minutes more.
6. Remove the skillet from the heat and transfer the cooked chicken to a bowl.
7. In a bowl, add all of the sauce ingredients and whisk well. Adjust the quantities of the ingredients until you get the consistency you desire.
8. On a platter, add the lettuce leaves, bowl of cooked chicken, and the bowl of sauce then serve immediately.

FISH AND VEGGIE STICKS

To make this crunchy lunch recipe, you will be using gluten-free breading. Children love fried foods, and parents like you love making easy dishes. Add a side of fresh veggie sticks and you have a winning dish that's fun, colorful, and healthy, too.

Time: 35 minutes

Serving Size: 5 servings

Prep Time: 15 minutes

Cook Time: 20 minutes

Ingredients:

- ½ tsp black pepper
- ½ tsp salt
- 1 tsp paprika
- 2 tbsp flax (ground)
- ¼ cup of coconut milk
- ¼ cup of Parmesan cheese
- ½ cup of all-purpose flour (gluten-free)
- 1 cup of bread crumbs (gluten-free)
- 1 lb cod fillets (cut into strips)
- ½ carrot (cut into strips)
- ½ cucumber (cut into strips)

Directions:

1. Preheat your oven to 425 F and use parchment paper to line a baking sheet.
2. In one bowl, add the flour. In a second bowl, add the coconut milk. And in a third bowl, add the flax, Parmesan cheese, bread crumbs, salt, pepper, and paprika, then mix well.
3. Dip a strip of cod into the flour, then into the coconut milk, then into the bread crumb mixture. Make sure you coat the whole strip of cod evenly with the bread crumb mixture.
4. Place the breaded strip of cod on the baking sheet and repeat the breading steps for the remaining strips.
5. Place the baking sheet in the oven and bake the fish sticks for about 20 minutes. Halfway through the cooking process, flip the fish sticks over.
6. Take the baking sheet out of the oven and transfer the fish sticks to a serving plate.
7. Add the veggie sticks to the plate and serve with your child's favorite dipping sauce.

RAINBOW RICE BOWL

This dish is filled with protein, vibrant colors, and a unique flavor. If you're looking to help your child become a more adventurous eater, this is a great dish to start with. You can even customize the ingredients to mix things up and serve this dish over and over again.

Time: 20 minutes

Serving Size: 6 servings

Prep Time: 10 minutes

Cook Time: 10 minutes

Ingredients:

- ¼ tsp pepper

- 1 tsp chili powder
- 1 tsp cumin (ground)
- 1 tsp salt
- 1 tbsp sugar
- ¼ cup of cilantro (fresh, minced)
- ¼ cup of red wine vinegar
- ½ cup of olive oil
- 1 ½ cups of corn (frozen, thawed)
- 2 cups of black beans (canned, rinsed, drained)
- 2 cups of kidney beans (canned, rinsed, drained)
- 3 cups of basmati rice (cooked)
- 1 clove of garlic (minced)
- 1 small sweet red pepper (chopped)
- 4 green onions (sliced)

Directions:

1. In a bowl, add the olive oil, red wine vinegar, sugar, garlic, salt, cumin, chili powder, and pepper. Whisk well.
2. Add the rest of the ingredients and toss until well combined.
3. Spoon the rainbow rice mixture into bowls and serve!

BLT LUNCHBOX

Children love bacon, so this tasty dish will surely be met with a lot of enthusiasm and excitement. Instead of serving your child a traditional BLT with bread that isn't gluten-free, prepare this yummy lunchbox for them. You can serve this at home or pack it for your child's school lunch.

Time: 15 minutes

Serving Size: 2 servings

Prep Time: 15 minutes

Cook Time: no cooking time

Ingredients for the lunchbox:

- ½ cup of mozzarella cheese (shredded)
- 1 cup of cherry tomatoes (cut in half)
- 4 cups of romaine lettuce (finely shredded)
- ½ avocado (diced)
- 4 slices of bacon (cooked until crispy, chopped)

Ingredients for the dressing:

- ½ tsp dill (dried)
- ½ tsp garlic powder

- 1 tbsp parsley (fresh, finely chopped)
- ¼ cup of mayonnaise
- ⅛ cup of milk
- Black pepper
- Salt

Directions:

1. Prepare 2 lunch boxes to assemble the ingredients.
2. Start by creating a bed of romaine lettuce in each lunch box.
3. Top with cherry tomatoes, cheese, bacon, and diced avocado.
4. In a bowl, add all of the dressing ingredients and mix well.
5. Drizzle the dressing over the lunch boxes and serve!

GRILLED TURKEY KABOBS

These turkey kabobs are tasty, healthy, and fun to eat. The turkey cubes are combined with other yummy ingredients then grilled to perfection. You can also swap the turkey in this recipe for chicken, if you prefer.

Time: 25 minutes

Serving Size: 4 servings

Prep Time: 15 minutes

Cook Time: 10 minutes

Ingredients:

- 1 tsp prepared mustard
- 2 tbsp canola oil
- 2 tbsp Worcestershire sauce
- ¼ cup of brown sugar
- 1 cup of pineapple chunks (canned, unsweetened)
- 1 lb turkey breast tenderloins (cut into cubes)
- 1 clove of garlic (minced)
- 1 large green pepper (cut into cubes)
- 1 large sweet onion (cut into cubes)
- 1 large sweet red pepper (cut into cubes)
- Cooking spray
- Metal or wooden skewers

Directions:

1. Drain the juice from the canned pineapple and set aside ¼ cup.
2. In a bowl, add the pineapple juice, garlic, oil, brown

sugar, Worcestershire sauce, and mustard, then mix well.
3. In another bowl, add the turkey cubes along with ⅓ cup of the marinade, and toss to coat.
4. Cover the bowl with cling wrap and place in the refrigerator for at least 2 hours.
5. Cover the bowl of the marinade with cling wrap, too, and place it in the refrigerator until it's time to cook.
6. Take out the bowl of marinated turkey cubes.
7. Use the skewers to thread the turkey cubes, pineapple chunks, and veggies alternately.
8. Lightly grease your grill with cooking spray and place the turkey kabobs on it.
9. Brush the turkey kabobs with the remaining marinade from the refrigerator, cover the grill, and cook the kabobs for about 8 to 10 minutes until the turkey cubes aren't pink anymore.
10. Turn the turkey kabobs occasionally and baste them frequently.
11. Once cooked, place the turkey kabobs on a platter and serve.

CHICKEN CAULI-RICE BOWL

These days, cauliflower rice is all the rage—and for good reason! It's delicious, healthy, and nutritious. These rice bowls are made with cauliflower rice along with other tasty ingredients to create an amazing dish that your child will enjoy. After serving this dish, watch as your child gobbles everything up!

Time: 6 hours and 10 minutes

Serving Size: 4 servings

Prep Time: 10 minutes

Cook Time: 6 hours

Ingredients:

- 1 tbsp oil
- ¼ cup of cilantro (chopped)
- ½ cup of black olives (sliced)
- ½ cup of guacamole
- 1 cup of cheddar cheese (shredded)
- 1 ½ cups of salsa (store-bought or homemade)
- 4 cups of riced cauliflower
- 1 lb chicken thighs (you can also use chicken breasts)

- Sour cream (for serving)

Directions:

1. In a slow cooker, add the salsa and chicken thighs.
2. Cook for about 4 hours on high or on low for about 6 hours.
3. Once cooked, shred the chicken using forks.
4. In a skillet, add the oil and riced cauliflower over medium-high heat.
5. Sauté the cauliflower for about 5 minutes, until tender and heated through.
6. Add the cilantro and mix well to combine.
7. Turn the heat off then start assembling the rice bowls.
8. Scoop the cauliflower rice in the bowls then top with chicken, salsa, olives, cheese, guacamole, and sour cream. Serve immediately!

CLASSIC SPAGHETTI AND GROUND MEATBALLS

Spaghetti and meatballs is a classic dish that's super popular with children. Fortunately, you can easily make this dish gluten-free simply by using the right ingredients. The great thing about this recipe is that you can prepare all of the ingredients at the same time so that the dish comes together wonderfully, too.

Time: 40 minutes

Serving Size: 3 servings

Prep Time: 10 minutes

Cook Time: 30 minutes

Ingredients:

- 2 tbsp olive oil (divided)

- ⅔ cups of Parmesan cheese (grated)
- 3 cups of marinara sauce (gluten-free)
- 1 lb ground beef (lean)
- 1 lb spaghetti (gluten-free)
- Black pepper
- Salt
- 1 tbsp basil (freshly chopped, optional)

Directions:

1. In a skillet, heat 1 tablespoon of olive oil over medium-high heat.
2. Add the beef and use a wooden spoon to brown. Break apart any lumps as needed.
3. Add the marinara sauce to the skillet, along with the basil if using.
4. Turn the heat down to medium and allow the sauce to simmer until heated through for about 15 minutes.
5. Season with salt and pepper as you are cooking the sauce.
6. Cook the spaghetti according to the directions on the packet.
7. Drain the water from the noodles, then add 1 tablespoon of oil and toss lightly.
8. Spoon the noodles onto platters, top with sauce,

sprinkle with Parmesan cheese, and serve while hot!

DECONSTRUCTED FISH TACOS

Tacos are fun and tasty no matter how you present them. If your child isn't a fan of fish, serve this dish to them and change their mind. These tacos are made with fresh ingredients and flaky fish for a wonderful combination of flavors and textures.

Time: 25 minutes

Serving Size: 2 servings

Prep Time: 15 minutes

Cook Time: 10 minutes

Ingredients:

- ¼ tsp black pepper (divided)
- ½ tsp cumin (ground)
- ½ tsp salt (divided)
- 1 tsp jalapeño pepper (seeded, chopped)
- 2 tsp lime juice
- 4 tsp canola oil (divided)
- ¼ cup of cilantro (fresh, chopped)

- 1 cup of coleslaw mix (homemade)
- ½ medium avocado (peeled, sliced)
- 1 green onion (sliced)
- 2 tilapia fillets (de-boned)

Directions:

1. In a bowl, add the coleslaw mix, cilantro, green onion, jalapeño pepper, lime juice, 2 teaspoons of oil, cumin, ¼ teaspoon of salt, and ⅛ teaspoon of pepper then toss lightly until well combined.
2. Place the bowl in the refrigerator to chill.
3. Use a paper towel to pat the tilapia fillets dry, then season with the rest of the salt and pepper.
4. In a skillet, heat the rest of the oil over medium-high heat.
5. Add the tilapia fillets and cook for about 3 to 4 minutes on each side.
6. Place the cooked tilapia fillets on a plate, then top with the chilled coleslaw mixture and some avocado.
7. Serve immediately.

BUILD YOUR OWN EGG CUPS

This recipe is perfect for breakfast, lunch, and even for snack time. It's rich in healthy fats, protein, and amazing flavors. The best part is, you can change the ingredients to make things more interesting for your child.

Time: 28 minutes

Serving Size: 24 mini egg cups

Prep Time: 10 minutes

Cook Time: 18 minutes

Ingredients:

- 3 tbsp milk
- ½ cup of pepperoni slices
- 1 cup of mozzarella cheese (shredded)
- 6 eggs
- Cooking spray

Directions:

1. Preheat your oven to 350 F and use cooking spray to grease a mini muffin pan.
2. In a bowl, add the milk and eggs. Whisk well.

3. Add the pepperoni slices and cheese, then continue whisking until all ingredients are well combined.
4. Carefully pour the mixture into the greased muffin pan.
5. Place the muffin pan in the oven and bake the egg cups for about 15 to 18 minutes.
6. Take the muffin pan out of the oven and allow the egg cups to cool down slightly before serving.

STEAK AND EGGS SALAD

Salads aren't just for people who want to lose weight. Serve this fancy dish to your child for a healthy and scrumptious lunch. This is a great way to add more veggies to your child's diet. You can even mix and match the veggies in this recipe to make different kinds of salads to pair with the rest of the ingredients.

Time: 30 minutes

Serving Size: 4 servings

Prep Time: 15 minutes

Cook Time: 15 minutes

Ingredients:

- ¼ tsp black pepper
- ½ tsp salt
- 1 tsp steak seasoning
- 2 tbsp butter (divided, you can also use coconut oil)
- ¼ cup of Parmesan cheese (shredded)
- 6 cups of baby spinach (fresh)
- 1 lb beef flank steak (you can also use skirt steak)
- 1 sweet red pepper (chopped)
- 1 yellow summer squash (sliced)
- 1 zucchini (sliced)
- 4 large eggs

Directions:

1. Rub the steak with the seasoning then place in a grill over medium heat.
2. Grill the steak for about 3 to 5 minutes, flip, then continue grilling for about 3 to 5 minutes more. Cook the steak to your desired level of doneness.
3. Once cooked, allow the steak to rest for about 5 minutes.
4. In a skillet, melt 1 tablespoon of butter over medium-high heat.
5. Add the squash, zucchini, and red pepper and cook for about 5 to 7 minutes.

6. Season with salt and pepper, then add the spinach, stir, and cook for about 2 minutes until wilted.
7. Spoon the veggie mixture onto serving plates.
8. Add the remaining butter to the skillet, along with the eggs. Cook the eggs according to your child's preference.
9. Slice the steak into thin strips and place the strips over the veggies.
10. Top each plate with an egg and Parmesan cheese. Serve immediately.

BEEF TACOS WITH AVOCADO

Now it's time for a more traditional dish. These tacos look like the classic tacos, but they use gluten-free ingredients. They're crunchy, filling, and contain a bunch of flavorful ingredients. Talk about a healthy and vibrant dish!

Time: 30 minutes

Serving Size: 3 servings

Prep Time: 20 minutes

Cook Time: 10 minutes

Ingredients:

- 1 tbsp olive oil
- 2 tbsp taco seasoning (gluten-free)
- 3 tbsp water
- ½ cup of avocado (chopped)
- ½ cup of red onions (finely chopped)
- 1 cup of mozzarella cheese (shredded)
- 2 cups of baby spinach (fresh, finely shredded)
- 1 lb lean ground beef
- 6 hard taco shells (gluten-free)

Directions:

1. Place the taco shells on a baking sheet.
2. Place the baking sheet in the oven and warm the taco shells for about 5 minutes at 350 F.
3. In a skillet, add the olive oil and ground beef over medium heat.
4. Brown the ground beef until completely cooked through.
5. Turn the heat down to low, then add the water and taco seasoning.
6. Allow the mixture to simmer for about 2 to 3 minutes, stirring occasionally.
7. Take the baking sheet out of the oven and start assembling the tacos.
8. Spoon ground beef at the bottom of each taco then

top with onion, avocado, and spinach.

9. Sprinkle cheese over each taco and serve!

BROILED CHICKEN DRUMSTICKS

These chicken drumsticks are healthy, yummy, and super easy to make. Although marinating these drumsticks may take some time, you can do this step in advance. That way, all you will have to do is broil the drumsticks when it's almost lunchtime. Easy peasy!

Time: 40 minutes

Serving Size: 4 servings

Prep Time: 10 minutes

Cook Time: 30 minutes

Ingredients:

- 1 tbsp brown sugar
- 2 tbsp red wine vinegar
- 2 tbsp soy sauce
- 3 tbsp olive oil
- 2 cloves of garlic
- 8 chicken drumsticks
- Black pepper

- Cooking spray
- Salt

Directions:

1. Preheat your oven to 425°F and use cooking spray to grease a baking sheet.
2. In a bowl, add all of the ingredients except the chicken drumsticks and whisk together well.
3. Pour the mixture into a Ziplock bag, then add the chicken drumsticks.
4. Shake the Ziplock bag to coat the chicken drumsticks, then place it in the refrigerator for a minimum of 30 minutes. The longer you wait, the more flavorful the chicken will be.
5. When you're ready to cook, take the Ziplock bag out of the refrigerator.
6. Transfer the chicken drumsticks to the baking sheet and discard the marinade.
7. Sprinkle the chicken drumsticks with a pinch of brown sugar.
8. Place the baking sheet into the oven and bake the chicken drumsticks for about 30 minutes.
9. Flip the chicken drumsticks, change the setting of your oven to low broil, and continue cooking for 10 more minutes.

10. Once cooked, take the baking sheet out of the oven and serve the chicken drumsticks with a healthy side dish.

STUFFED AVOCADO BOATS

These avocado boats are healthy, filling, and go well with a side of rice, beans or even gluten-free chips. Whether chilled or straight from the oven, this tasty dish will make your child's lunch experience more enjoyable.

Time: 20 minutes

Serving Size: 8 servings

Prep Time: 10 minutes

Cook Time: 10 minutes

Ingredients:

- ¼ tsp black pepper
- ½ tsp paprika
- 1 tbsp capers (drained)
- 2 tbsp chives (minced)
- 2 tbsp lemon juice
- 4 tbsp cilantro (fresh, chopped, divided)
- ½ cup of mayonnaise

- 1 cup of pepper jack cheese (shredded)
- 1 ½ cups of lump crabmeat (canned, drained)
- 1 Serrano pepper (seeded, minced)
- 5 avocados (peeled, halved)
- Cooking spray
- Lemon wedges (for serving)

Directions:

1. Preheat your broiler and use cooking spray to grease a baking pan.
2. In a bowl, add 2 avocado halves and use a fork to mash lightly.
3. Add lemon juice and mayonnaise, then mix well.
4. Add the crab meat, chives, capers, black pepper, Serrano pepper, and 3 tablespoons of cilantro, then continue mixing.
5. Spoon the mixture into the rest of the avocado halves and transfer them to the baking pan. Top each avocado half with paprika and cheese.
6. Place the baking pan into the oven and broil for 4 to 5 minutes.
7. Take the baking pan out of the oven and sprinkle each avocado half with cilantro.
8. Serve with lemon wedges and a healthy side dish.

CUBAN-STYLE PICADILLO

This delicious recipe has a unique taste that will leave your child feeling pleasantly surprised. It contains a mix of ingredients that are healthy, filling, and fit right into your child's diet. It's the perfect dish for when your child is feeling adventurous.

Time: 25 minutes

Serving Size: 4 servings

Prep Time: 15 minutes

Cook Time: 10 minutes

Ingredients:

- 1 tsp olive oil
- 1 tbsp apple cider vinegar
- ¼ cup of onion (chopped)
- ¼ cup of raisins
- ½ cup of pimiento-stuffed olives (sliced)
- 1 cup of tomato sauce
- 2 cups of rice (cooked)
- 1 lb lean ground beef
- 1 green pepper (chopped)
- Cilantro leaves (fresh, for topping)

Directions:

1. In a skillet, warm the oil over medium heat.
2. Add the pepper, onion, and beef, then cook for about 5 to 7 minutes.
3. Add the tomato sauce, vinegar, raisins, and olives. Mix well and bring to a boil.
4. Once boiling, turn the heat down to low and allow to simmer for about 5 to 6 minutes.
5. Scoop the picadillo into bowls and top with cilantro.
6. Serve immediately with a side of hot rice.

GRAIN-FREE LUNCH WRAPS

This is another versatile recipe that you can make in different ways. You can follow it precisely, add, remove or change the ingredients, or even use leftovers for the filling. This simple recipe is easy to make but it will surely make lunchtime more enjoyable for your child.

Time: 25 minutes

Serving Size: 4 servings

Prep Time: 15 minutes

Cook Time: 10 minutes

Ingredients for the wrap:

- ¼ tsp garlic salt (can omit for sweet fillings)
- ¼ tsp nutritional yeast
- ½ tsp salt
- ¼ cup of almond milk (you can also use other types of milk)
- ¼ cup of coconut flour
- 6 eggs (whites only)
- Cooking spray

Ingredients for the filling:

- ½ cup of cheese (shredded)
- ½ cup of lettuce leaves (shredded)
- 1 cup of quinoa (cooked)
- 8 slices of bacon (cooked)
- 8 tomato slices

Directions:

1. In a blender, add all of the wrap ingredients and process at low speed until you get a smooth consistency.
2. Allow the batter to sit for about 10 minutes.

3. Grease a skillet with cooking spray over medium heat.
4. Pour ¼ cup of batter into the skillet and swirl it around to spread evenly.
5. Cook the wrap for about 1 minute, flip it, then cook for 30 seconds more.
6. Once cooked, transfer the wrap to a plate.
7. Repeat the cooking steps until you have used up all of the batter.
8. Scoop some cooked quinoa onto one of the wraps and top with lettuce, tomato slices, bacon strips, and cheese.
9. Wrap and serve!

SKILLET SHRIMP WITH FETA

Seafood is a healthy addition to any diet, even a gluten-free one. With this dish, your child will become more interested in trying seafood. This is a yummy meal that's simple to cook and can be ready in half an hour. Whip up a big batch so you can have some, too!

Time: 30 minutes

Serving Size: 4 servings

Prep Time: 10 minutes

Cook Time: 20 minutes

Ingredients:

- ¼ tsp salt
- ½ tsp black pepper
- 1 tsp oregano (dried)
- 1 tbsp olive oil
- 2 tbsp parsley (fresh, minced)
- ¾ cup of feta cheese (crumbled)
- 3 cups of tomatoes (canned, diced)
- 1 lb medium shrimp (uncooked, peeled, deveined)
- 1 onion (finely chopped)
- 3 cloves of garlic (minced)

Directions:

1. In a skillet, warm the olive oil over medium-high heat.
2. Add the onion and cook until tender, for about 4 to 6 minutes.
3. Add the garlic, oregano, salt, and pepper, then continue cooking for 1 minute more.
4. Add the tomatoes, mix well, and bring to a boil.
5. Once boiling, turn the heat down to medium and allow to simmer for about 5 to 7 minutes until the sauce thickens slightly.

6. Add the parsley and shrimp, then continue cooking for about 5 to 6 minutes while stirring occasionally.
7. Take the skillet off the heat and top with cheese.
8. Cover the skillet with a lid for about 5 minutes until the cheese softens.
9. Serve with a side of veggies or rice.

HEARTY VEGETABLE SOUP

This hearty soup is fresh, easy, and quick to make. It has a subtle flavor and a creamy texture, making it super comforting. Prepare this dish when the weather is cold and it will warm your child up right away. Serve it with a side of gluten-free crackers or chips for a filling lunch.

Time: 40 minutes

Serving Size: 8 servings

Prep Time: 20 minutes

Cook Time: 20 minutes

Ingredients:

- 2 tsp salt
- 1 tbsp onion powder
- 3 tbsp amaranth flour
- 3 tbsp butter (you can also use olive oil)
- 1 ½ cups of cream
- 3 cups of mixed vegetables (fresh, chopped)
- 3 ½ cups of chicken broth (gluten-free)
- 1 clove of garlic (minced)
- White pepper (fresh cracked)

Directions:

1. Steam the veggies until tender and cooked, then set aside.
2. In a stockpot, warm the butter over medium heat.
3. Add the amaranth flour and whisk well until you form a paste.
4. Add the garlic and keep whisking for about 1 minute until the mixture is bubbly and smooth.
5. Add the chicken broth gradually while you continue whisking. Do this until you get a creamy and smooth mixture.
6. Add the cream, salt, onion powder, white pepper, and the steamed veggies then mix until smooth.

7. Take the stockpot off the heat and allow the mixture to cool for about 10 minutes.
8. Transfer the mixture into a blender until you get a smooth texture that's free of lumps.
9. Pour the vegetable soup into serving bowls and serve with crackers, chips, or any other side dish of your choice.

GRILLED PORK CHOPS

These pork chops are moist, flavorful, and super healthy. If you want to serve your child with an elegant dish, this is an excellent choice. It's easy and quick to make, it's gluten-free, and it goes perfectly with different kinds of side dishes.

Time: 25 minutes

Serving Size: 6 servings

Prep Time: 10 minutes

Cook Time: 15 minutes

Ingredients for the pork chops:

- 4 tsp cumin (ground)
- 2 tbsp olive oil
- ¼ cup of jalapeño peppers (seeded, finely chopped)

- ½ cup of lime juice
- ½ cup of sweet onion (chopped)
- 1 ½ lbs pork chops
- Cooking spray

Ingredients for the salsa:

- ¼ tsp black pepper
- ¼ tsp salt
- 1 tbsp honey
- 2 tbsp cilantro (fresh, minced)
- 1 cucumber (seeded, chopped)
- 2 avocados (peeled, chopped)
- 2 green onions (chopped)
- 2 plum tomatoes (seeded, chopped)

Directions:

1. In a bowl, add the cumin, olive oil, jalapeño peppers, and lime juice. Mix well.
2. Take ⅓ of the marinade and set aside.
3. Add the pork chops then toss to coat.
4. Cover the bowl with cling wrap and place in the refrigerator for a minimum of 30 minutes. The longer you wait, the more flavorful the pork chops will be.

5. In a saucepan, add the reserved marinade and bring to a boil.
6. Allow to simmer while stirring for about 1 to 2 minutes until it thickens slightly.
7. Take the saucepan off the heat.
8. In a bowl, add all of the salsa ingredients along with the thickened marinade.
9. Toss everything lightly to coat.
10. Take the pork chops out of the oven and drain the marinade.
11. Preheat your grill then grease it lightly with cooking spray.
12. Place the pork chops on the grill and cook for about 4 to 5 minutes on each side.
13. Once cooked, transfer the pork chops to plates, and serve with homemade salsa.

THAI-STYLE NOODLE SOUP BOWL

These peanut-flavored noodles are nutty, healthy, and savory. The noodles themselves have a chewy texture, which is perfect when combined with the special sauce. You can make this dish even more filling by adding ingredients like chicken or seafood. Either way, these noodles will surely be a hit with your whole family.

Time: 25 minutes

Serving Size: 3 servings

Prep Time: 15 minutes

Cook Time: 10 minutes

Ingredients for the noodles:

- 2 tsp sesame oil
- 1 tbsp sesame seeds
- 2 tbsp vegetable oil
- 3 tbsp soy sauce
- ½ cup of basil (fresh)
- 1 cup of tofu (firm, cubed)
- 2 cups of bean sprouts
- 2 cups of rice noodles (cooked)
- 3 green onions (sliced)

Ingredients for the sauce:

- ½ tsp cayenne pepper
- 1 tsp tamarind paste
- 1 tbsp soy sauce
- 3 tbsp brown sugar
- ¾ cup of water (hot)
- 1 cup of peanuts (unsalted, dry-roasted)
- 3 cloves of garlic

Directions:

1. In a bowl, add the tofu and soy sauce. Toss to combine then set aside to marinate.
2. In a separate bowl, add the hot water and tamarind paste. Mix well until the paste dissolves completely.
3. Add into a blender along with all the other sauce ingredients.
4. Blend until you get a smooth consistency.
5. In a wok, warm the oil over medium-high heat.
6. Add the tofu and stir-fry until cooked and lightly browned.
7. Transfer the tofu into a bowl and set aside.
8. Place the wok back on the stove and add more oil.
9. Add the cooked noodles and stir-fry for about 1 minute.
10. Add $1/3$ of the sauce, along with the tofu cubes, then continue stir-frying until the noodles are completely coated with sauce.
11. Add the bean sprouts with another of $1/3$ sauce and continue stir-frying.
12. Drizzle with sesame oil and sprinkle with sesame seeds.
13. Transfer the noodles into bowls. Top with basil and green onions and serve hot.

SKILLET CHILI

There's nothing like a hearty bowl of chili for lunch. This recipe has veggies, meat, and cheese, making it an amazingly filling and tasty dish. Have a bowl or two with your child while you share stories and enjoy your time together.

Time: 55 minutes

Serving Size: 4 servings

Prep Time: 15 minutes

Cook Time: 40 minutes

Ingredients:

- 1 tsp olive oil
- 1 tsp oregano (dried)
- 1 tsp salt
- 3 tsp chili powder
- ½ cup of long grain rice (uncooked)
- ½ cup of green pepper (chopped)
- ½ cup of olives (ripe, sliced)
- ½ cup of water
- 1 cup of cheddar cheese (shredded, you can also use Monterey Jack cheese)
- 1 cup of corn (frozen or canned)

- 1 cup of onion (chopped)
- 1 cup of tomato juice
- 2 cups of kidney beans (canned, rinsed, drained)
- 1 lb ground beef
- 1 clove of garlic (minced)

Directions:

1. In a skillet, warm the olive oil over medium heat.
2. Add the beef, pepper, onion, and garlic until the meat is cooked through.
3. Drain excess liquid, then add the kidney beans, tomato juice, water, chili powder, oregano, salt, and rice. Mix well.
4. Cover the skillet with a lid and allow the mixture to simmer for about 25 minutes until the rice is cooked and tender.
5. Add the olives and corn, then continue cooking for about 5 minutes more.
6. Sprinkle with cheese, cover, and continue simmering for about 5 minutes more.
7. Spoon the chili into bowls and serve while hot.

CONCLUSION: HEALTHY, GLUTEN-FREE RECIPES FOR YOUR CHILD

Helping your child go gluten-free is right within your reach. Now that you have reached the end of this book, you already have all of the fundamental knowledge you need to guide your child into the gluten-free diet. From start to finish, you have learned a wealth of information here. In the first chapter, you learned all about celiac disease. The knowledge you gained will help you understand your child's condition more while dispelling the common misconceptions about the disease. In this chapter, you learned what celiac disease is, a few interesting (and sometimes unknown) facts about the disease, and even other types of autoimmune diseases that can potentially develop if celiac is left unchecked or untreated.

In Chapter 2, we dived deeper into the gluten-free diet. For you to make the best decision for yourself and your child,

CONCLUSION: HEALTHY, GLUTEN-FREE RECIPES FOR YO...

knowing both sides of the story is key. While hearing good things about a diet will make you feel more encouraged to follow it, not knowing the downsides and risks won't help you out in the long run. Imagine what would happen if you didn't know about the risk of nutrient deficiencies while on the gluten-free diet. You wouldn't know how to avoid this risk by learning how to balance your child's diet. In this chapter, you learned all about the benefits and downsides of the gluten-free diet, along with important information to make it easier for you to look out for the common signs and symptoms of celiac disease.

The next chapter was all about child empowerment. Since the gluten-free diet will be a permanent part of your child's life to manage their condition, they should know how to follow this diet even when you're not around to guide them. This chapter was filled with practical information to help you guide your child as they transition to the diet—and stick with it long-term. In the last three chapters, we discussed three important meals your child has each day: breakfast, snacks, and lunch. The chapters focused on the meals themselves along with a number of healthy, tasty, and super easy recipes that you can start making for your child. Mix and match these recipes to make the diet more interesting and enjoyable for your child. After practicing these easy recipes, you can move on to more complex dishes that take more time and effort to prepare.

CONCLUSION: HEALTHY, GLUTEN-FREE RECIPES FOR YO...

As promised at the beginning of this book, you are now armed with enough practical knowledge to help your child embark on their gluten-free diet journey. As a parent, one of the best things you can do for your child is to guide them until they are knowledgeable and strong enough to follow the diet on their own. Although finding out that your child suffers from celiac disease can be very frustrating and overwhelming, preparing and planning for it will make things much easier for you. People of all ages all around the world suffer from this disease, which means that you (and your child) aren't alone. I am also a sufferer of this condition and by educating myself, I have risen to the challenge. Now, I am an ardent follower of the gluten-free diet—and I couldn't be happier about it.

Before you go, I would like to thank you for choosing my book to help you learn about celiac disease and the gluten-free diet. I hope that you have achieved the enlightenment you need to help your child. It's time to change your perspective about celiac disease. Adapting a positive attitude will allow you to make the best plan for your child. And if you feel like this book changed your life for the better, I would appreciate it greatly if you could leave a positive review on Amazon. That way, other people looking for answers to help their child who suffers from celiac disease can also get the information and tips they need. Now, it's time for you to create a plan for your child to start transitioning to a gluten-free diet. Good luck!

REFERENCES

Academy of Nutrition and Dietetics. (2018). *Does My Child Need a Gluten Free Diet?* Eat Right. https://www.eatright.org/food/nutrition/vegetarian-and-special-diets/does-my-child-need-a-gluten-free-diet

Adams, J. (2019, October 16). *Ten Amazing Facts About Celiac Disease.* Celiac.Com. https://www.celiac.com/articles.html/ten-amazing-facts-about-celiac-disease-r4947/

Alderson, E. (2014, June 9). *Gluten Free Oat Crepes with Tomato, Basil, and Goat Cheese.* Naturally Ella. https://naturallyella.com/gluten-free-oat-crepes-with-tomatoes-basil-and-goat-cheese/

Axworthy, N. (2016a, October 20). *Cheesy Oats with Tomato, Avocado and Spinach.* Nature's Path. https://

REFERENCES

www.naturespath.com/en-us/recipes/cheesy-oats-tomato-avocado-spinach/

Axworthy, N. (2016b, December 22). *Sweet Potato Spice Smoothie Bowl*. Nature's Path. https://www.naturespath.com/en-us/recipes/sweet-potato-spice-smoothie-bowl/

Baines, E., & Blatchford, P. (2012, July 24). *Let's Do (School) Lunch: Lessons in Social and Emotional Development Can Never Replace the Real Thing*. IOE London Blog. https://ioelondonblog.wordpress.com/2012/07/24/lets-do-school-lunch-lessons-in-social-and-emotional-development-can-never-replace-the-real-thing/

Ballantyne, S. (2013, April 20). *Gluten-Free Diets Can Be Healthy for Kids*. The Paleo Mom. https://www.thepaleomom.com/gluten-free-diets-can-be-healthy-for-kids/

Barnes, A. (2017, June 6). *School Lunch is About More Than Serving Food, It's About School Culture*. We Are Teachers. https://www.weareteachers.com/importance-of-school-lunch/

Belluz, J. (2015, April 30). *The Gluten-Free Craze is Out of Hand. Here are 8 Facts to Counter the Madness*. Vox. https://www.vox.com/2015/4/30/8517749/gluten-free-diet-nutrition-celiac-disease

REFERENCES

Benthin, F. (2020). *Avocado Crab Boats*. Taste of Home. https://www.tasteofhome.com/recipes/avocado-crab-boats/

Beyond Celiac. (n.d.-a). *Baked Corn Dogs*. Beyond Celiac. https://www.beyondceliac.org/gluten-free-recipes/baked-corn-dogs/

Beyond Celiac. (n.d.-b). *Berry Yogurt Parfaits with Cherry-Almond Granola*. Beyond Celiac. https://www.beyondceliac.org/gluten-free-recipes/berry-yogurt-parfaits-with-cherry-almond-granola/

Beyond Celiac. (n.d.-c). *Brownie-Bottom Pumpkin Bars*. Beyond Celiac. https://www.beyondceliac.org/gluten-free-recipes/brownie-bottom-pumpkin-bars/

Beyond Celiac. (n.d.-d). *Butternut Squash Pizza | BeyondCeliac.org*. Beyond Celiac. https://www.beyondceliac.org/gluten-free-recipes/butternut-squash-pizza/

Beyond Celiac. (n.d.-e). *Candy Corn Mini Muffins*. Beyond Celiac. https://www.beyondceliac.org/gluten-free-recipes/candy-corn-mini-muffins/

Bjarnadottir, A. (2016, September 29). *The 14 Most Common Signs of Gluten Intolerance*. Healthline. https://www.healthline.com/nutrition/signs-you-are-gluten-intolerant

REFERENCES

Bodenner, C. (2016, May 17). *On the Risks and Benefits of a Gluten-Free Diet*. The Atlantic. https://www.theatlantic.com/notes/2016/05/the-harm-in-blindly-going-gluten-free-contd/483096/?gclid=Cj0KCQjw7sz6BRDYARIsAPHzrNKPggesSGWapcqojupQ44K6QE6M0PLGGXn5ywi49pVS8JWnh9BeQzkaAibcEALw_wcB

Bonder, M. J., Tigchelaar, E. F., Cai, X., Trynka, G., Cenit, M. C., Hrdlickova, B., Zhong, H., Vatanen, T., Gevers, D., Wijmenga, C., Wang, Y., & Zhernakova, A. (2016). The influence of a short-term gluten-free diet on the human gut microbiome. *Genome Medicine*, *8*(1). https://doi.org/10.1186/s13073-016-0295-y

Booth, S. (2017). *Should Your Child Go Gluten-Free?* WebMD. https://www.webmd.com/parenting/raising-fit-kids/food/features/should-kids-go-gluten-free#1

Bramkamp, E. (n.d.). *Naked Fish Tacos*. Taste of Home. https://www.tasteofhome.com/recipes/naked-fish-tacos/

Brazier, Y. (2020, January 28). *Gluten intolerance: Symptoms and intolerance vs. allergy*. Medical News Today. https://www.medicalnewstoday.com/articles/312898

Brianne. (2015, January 13). *Chocolate Pudding "Snack Hack."* Cupcakes & Kale Chips. https://cupcakesandkalechips.com/chocolate-pudding-snack-hack/

Brianne. (2018, November 6). *Sweet Chocolate Chip Pumpkin Hummus*. Cupcakes & Kale Chips. https://cupcakesandkalechips.com/sweet-pumpkin-hummus/

Brianne. (2019a, June 24). *Easy Cheesy Baked Cauliflower Tots Recipe*. Cupcakes & Kale Chips. https://cupcakesandkalechips.com/baked-cauli-tots/

Brianne. (2020a, January 7). *Cheesy Veggie Quinoa Bites*. Cupcakes & Kale Chips. https://cupcakesandkalechips.com/cheesy-veggie-quinoa-bites/

Brown, K. (2020). *Chili Skillet*. Taste of Home. https://www.tasteofhome.com/recipes/chili-skillet/

Celiac Disease Foundation. (2016, October 14). *20 Things You Might Not Know About Celiac Disease*. Celiac Disease Foundation. https://celiac.org/about-the-foundation/featured-news/2016/08/20-things-you-might-not-know-about-celiac-disease/

Celiac Disease Foundation. (2017, December 31). *What is Celiac Disease?* Celiac Disease Foundation. https://celiac.org/about-celiac-disease/what-is-celiac-disease/

Child Mind Institute. (n.d.). *12 Tips to Raise Confident Children | Building Self-Esteem*. Child Mind Institute. https://childmind.org/article/12-tips-raising-confident-kids/

REFERENCES

Clevenger, C. (n.d.). *The Hard Part Of Being a Celiac and Living a Gluten-Free Life*. Celeste's Best. http://www.celestesbest.com/blog/the-hard-part-of-being-a-celiac-and-living-a-gluten-free-life-/8deb09bf-44e3-a8e2-97bb-53d7bdf99b7a

Coconut, S. (2020). *Gluten Free Blueberry Muffins with Almond Crumble*. Driscoll's. https://www.driscolls.com/recipe/gluten-free-blueberry-muffins-with-almond-crumble

Darcey, M. (2017, November 22). *The Growth of Gluten Sensitivity and the Genetics Behind It - Pathway Genomics*. Pathway Genomics. https://www.pathway.com/blog/the-growth-of-gluten-sensitivity-and-the-genetics-behind-it/

Dash, T. (2013, August 6). *Raising Happy Gluten-Free Kids*. Boulder Locavore. https://boulderlocavore.com/best-tips-for-raising-happy-gluten-free-kids/

Deakin University. (n.d.). *Breakfast*. Better Health. https://www.betterhealth.vic.gov.au/health/healthyliving/:~:text=Breakfast%20is%20often%20called%20'the,nutrients%20required%20for%20good%20health.

Dean, K. (2015, February 11). *Sticky Bun Chia Seed Pudding*. I Heart Eating. https://www.ihearteating.com/sticky-bun-chia-seed-pudding/

Del Immune. (2018, June 27). *Autoimmune Disease Guide: What is Autoimmune Disease? Lists, Symptoms*. Del-Immune V. https://www.delimmune.com/2018/06/autoimmune-disease-guide/#impacts

Deskin, R. (2020). *Vegetable, Steak and Eggs*. Taste of Home. https://www.tasteofhome.com/recipes/vegetable-steak-and-eggs/

Duane, J. (2018, January 11). *The Media Encourages Negative Social Behavior Towards Gluten-Free Dieters*. Celiac.Com. https://www.celiac.com/articles.html/the-media-encourages-negative-social-behavior-towards-gluten-free-dieters-r4319/

Editorial Staff. (2018, February 27). *What Parents of Gluten-Free Kids Should Know*. Gluten Free & More. https://www.glutenfreeandmore.com/blog/six-things-parents-with-gluten-free-kids-should-know/

Eigler, H. (2015). *Peanut Butter and Honey Protein Pancakes*. Home to Heather. https://hometoheather.com/2015/03/peanut-butter-and-honey-protein-pancakes/

Fernandes, A. (2019, June 28). *10 Supercharged Health Benefits of Eating a Gluten-Free Diet*. Gluten-Free Living. https://www.glutenfreeliving.com/gluten-free-foods/diet/benefits-of-gluten-free-diet/

REFERENCES

FindMeCure Team. (2019, January 15). *5 Early Signs Of Autoimmune Disease*. FindMeCure. https://www.findmecure.com/blog/5-early-signs-of-autoimmune-disease/

Foley, M. (2014, July 7). *The Breakfast That Jessica Simpson Credits For Her Weight-Loss Success*. POPSUGAR Fitness. https://www.popsugar.com/fitness/Jessica-Simpson-Breakfast-35170922

Fotolia.com, B. J. F., LCSW, LICSW, CGP; Photo: (2020). *Teens Click with Their Cliques - Understanding an Adolescent Phenomenon*. Calgary's Child Magazine. https://www.calgarychild.com/parenting/parent-connection/2010-teens-click-with-their-cliques-understanding-an-adolescent-phenomenon

Fuentes, L. (2019, February 9). *Salsa Chicken Cauliflower Rice Bowls*. Laura Fuentes. https://www.laurafuentes.com/chicken-cauliflower-rice-bowls/

GI Kids. (2019). *Living with celiac disease*. Gi Kids. https://gikids.org/celiac-disease/coping/

Gluten Intolerance Group. (2019, October 17). *Associated Autoimmune Diseases*. Gluten Intolerance Group. https://gluten.org/2019/10/17/associated-autoimmune-diseases/#:~:text=The%20autoimmune%20conditions%20most%20associated

REFERENCES

Gluten-Free Therapeutics. (2014, December 16). *The Social Side of Living with Celiac Disease*. Gluten Free Therapeutics. https://www.glutenfreetherapeutics.com/living-gluten-free/medicine-research/social-side-living-celiac-disease/

Goodman, T. (n.d.). *Turkey Pepper Kabobs*. Taste of Home. https://www.tasteofhome.com/recipes/turkey-pepper-kabobs/

Gruss, T. (2019a, August 5). *Kid-Friendly, Gluten-Free Weeknight Spaghetti Recipe*. The Spruce Eats. https://www.thespruceeats.com/kid-friendly-gluten-free-spaghetti-1451037

Gruss, T. (2019b, September 25). *Gluten-Free Beef and Avocado Tacos Recipe*. The Spruce Eats. https://www.thespruceeats.com/gluten-free-tacos-with-avocado-1451045

Gruss, T. (2019c, November 9). *5 Gluten-Free Cream of Vegetable Soups*. The Spruce Eats. https://www.thespruceeats.com/gluten-free-cream-of-vegetable-soup-recipes-1451478

Hamblin, J. (2016, May 16). *The Harm in Blindly Going Gluten Free*. The Atlantic. https://www.theatlantic.com/science/archive/2016/05/celiac-vs-gluten/482676/?gclid=CjwKCAjwkdL6BRAREiwA-kiczLelADBRJpo4XT5AM4VNg3I4l5nOEYf-V656qfLFRzUoaEmnWWAXohoC0XkQAvD_BwE

REFERENCES

Handwerk, B. (2018, March 13). *How Cheese, Wheat and Alcohol Shaped Human Evolution*. Smithsonian. https://www.smithsonianmag.com/science-nature/how-cheese-wheat-and-alcohol-shaped-human-evolution-180968455/

Harvard Health Publishing. (2019). *7 Ways to Snack Smarter*. Harvard Health. https://www.health.harvard.edu/staying-healthy/7-ways-to-snack-smarter

Harvard T.H. Chan. (2017, May 23). *Gluten: A Benefit or Harm to the Body?* The Nutrition Source. https://www.hsph.harvard.edu/nutritionsource/gluten/#:~:text=When%20Gluten%20Is%20a%20Problem&text=The%20side%20effects%20can%20range

Haynes, H. (2014, June 28). *Sweet Potato French Toast*. Kula Mama. https://kulamama.com/sweet-potato-french-toast/

Haynes, H. (2015, April 6). *Freezer Protein Bars for Kids*. Kula Mama. https://kulamama.com/freezer-protein-bars-for-kids/

Healtheries. (n.d.). *The Importance of Healthy Snacking for Kids*. Healtheries. https://healtheries.co.nz/articles/the-importance-of-healthy-snacking-for-kids

Healthy Food Choices in Schools. (2019, June 12). *How Peer and Parental Influences Affect Meal Choices*. Healthy

Food Choices in Schools. https://healthy-food-choices-in-schools.extension.org/how-peer-and-parental-influences-affect-meal-choices/

Help Your Child Feel Good About Himself. (n.d.). YES Safe Choices. http://www.yessafechoices.org/parents/tips-and-tools/help-your-child-feel-good-about-himself

Hunn, N. (2014, August 20). *No Bake Gluten Free Granola Bars.* No Bake Gluten on a Shoestring. https://glutenfreeonashoestring.com/no-bake-gluten-free-granola-bars/

Jegtvig, S. (2020, April 16). *6 Ways You Can Help Gluten-Free Kids Cope With School.* Verywell Health. https://www.verywellhealth.com/help-gluten-free-kids-cope-in-school-562511

Jordan, P. (2013, January 20). *Baked Gluten Free Mozzarella Sticks.* I'm A Celiac. http://www.imaceliac.com/2013/01/baked-gluten-free-mozzarella-sticks.html

Joy, E. (2019, April 10). *5 Ways to Raise a Healthy, Confident Gluten-Free Kid.* Gluten-Free Living. https://www.glutenfreeliving.com/gluten-free-lifestyle/kids/5-ways-to-raise-a-healthy-confident-gluten-free-kid/

Kannall, E. (2018, December 9). *Does Gluten Make You Tired?* SF Gate. https://healthyeating.sfgate.com/gluten-make-tired-8804.html

Kelly, K. (2015, April 14). *Easiest Five Ingredient Chicken Drumsticks (Gluten Free).* Seasonal Cravings. https://www.seasonalcravings.com/easiest-five-ingredient-chicken-drumsticks/

Kelly, K. (2016, March 14). *Chicken Lettuce Wraps.* Seasonal Cravings. https://www.seasonalcravings.com/chicken-lettuce-wraps/

Kids Health. (2015). *Celiac Disease.* KidsHealth.Org. https://kidshealth.org/en/kids/celiac.html

Kleinworth & Co. (2020, April 16). *Homemade Potato Chips.* Kleinworth & Co. https://www.kleinworthco.com/homemade-potato-chips/

Krampf, M. (2018, January 13). *Baked Cheddar Parmesan Crisps Recipe.* Wholesome Yum. https://www.wholesomeyum.com/recipes/baked-cheddar-parmesan-crisps-recipe/

Kuzemchak, S. (2014, April 27). *The Benefits of Going Gluten-Free.* Parents. https://www.parents.com/health/allergies/food/going-gluten-free/

REFERENCES

Laura. (2013, November 15). *Gluten Free Vegan Animal Graham Crackers*. Petite Allergy Treats. https://petiteallergytreats.com/gluten-free-vegan-animal-graham-crackers/

Laura. (2014, July 24). *Grain Free Lunchbox Wraps Recipe*. MOMables. https://www.momables.com/grain-free-lunchbox-wraps-recipe/

Laura. (2019b, March 28). *3 Healthy Breakfast Egg Cups*. MOMables. https://www.momables.com/how-to-make-egg-cups/

Laura. (2019c, May 16). *Homemade Gluten Free Fish Sticks*. MOMables. https://www.momables.com/allergy-friendly-homemade-fish-sticks/

Laura. (2019d, June 13). *BLT Salad Meal Prep*. MOMables. https://www.momables.com/blt-salad-lunch/

Layne, A. (2012, June 19). *Quinoa Omelette Breakfast Cups*. DAMY Health. https://www.damyhealth.com/2012/06/quinoa-omelette-breakfast-cups/

Lee, A. R. (2015). *Impact of Social Support Networks on Quality of Life in Celiac Disease*. Manitoba Celiac. https://www.manitobaceliac.com/wp-content/uploads/2015/06/lee.pdf

REFERENCES

Lee, J. (n.d.). *Cool Beans Salad*. Taste of Home. https://www.tasteofhome.com/recipes/cool-beans-salad/

Lee, J. L. (2014, April 26). *Mini Mediterranean Gluten Free Quiche*. Jesse Lane Wellness. https://www.jesselanewellness.com/recipes/gluten-free-quiche/

Leger, A. (2011, June 30). *10 Tips to Empower Celiac Children to Live Gluten Free*. The Savvy Celiac. http://www.thesavvyceliac.com/2011/06/30/10-ways-to-empower-celiac-children-to-live-gluten-free/

Leger, A. (2015, May 1). *Gluten-Free in the Media Spotlight: Does That Glare Help or Hurt?* Gluten-Free Living. https://www.glutenfreeliving.com/blog/gluten-free-media/

Lerner, A., O'Bryan, T., & Matthias, T. (2019, October 15). *Navigating the Gluten-Free Boom: The Dark Side of Gluten Free Diet*. Frontiers in Pediatrics. https://www.frontiersin.org/articles/10.3389/fped.2019.00414/full

Levine Finke, J. (2018, May 1). *12 Little Known Facts About Celiac Disease*. Good For You Gluten Free. https://www.goodforyouglutenfree.com/facts-about-celiac-disease/

Ludwig, E. (2019, November 27). *Overview of Fatigue Caused by Gluten*. Verywell Health. https://www.verywellhealth.com/fatigue-caused-by-gluten-how-you-can-cope-562318#:~:text=One%20study%20found%20that%2082

Mayo Clinic Staff. (2017). *Nutrition for Kids: Guidelines for a Healthy Diet*. Mayo Clinic. https://www.mayoclinic.org/healthy-lifestyle/childrens-health/in-depth/nutrition-for-kids/art-20049335

McEvoy, C. (2012, May 23). *5 Tips to Empower Gluten-Free Kids*. Celiac Central: Bits and Bites. https://celiaccentral.wordpress.com/2012/05/23/5-tips-to-empower-gluten-free-kids/

McKenney, S. (2013, June 19). *Breakfast Cookies*. Sally's Baking Addiction. https://sallysbakingaddiction.com/breakfast-cookies/

Minimalist Baker. (2014, March 29). *Healthy Chocolate Chip Oatmeal Cookie Pancakes*. Minimalist Baker. https://minimalistbaker.com/chocolate-chip-oatmeal-cookie-pancakes-2-0/

Mueller, B. (2016, September 6). *Grilled Fruit Salad*. Nature's Path. https://www.naturespath.com/en-us/recipes/grilled-fruit-salad/

Mueller, B. (2017, April 27). *Caramelized Banana Oatmeal*. Nature's Path. https://www.naturespath.com/en-ca/recipes/caramelized-banana-oatmeal/

REFERENCES

Mullins, B. (2018, January 29). *How to Stop Mindless Snacking, FINALLY*. Eating Bird Food. https://www.eatingbirdfood.com/how-to-stop-mindless-snacking/

Myers, G. (2012, July 4). *An Evolutionary Explanation for Gluten Intolerance*. Celiac.Com. https://www.celiac.com/articles.html/an-evolutionary-explanation-for-gluten-intolerance-r2457/

Natalie. (2020b, July 22). *Soft Pretzel Bites*. Super Healthy Kids. https://www.superhealthykids.com/recipes/soft-pretzel-bites-allergy-free/

Nature's Path. (2016, March 18). *Pumped Up Muesli Chia Pudding*. Nature's Path. https://www.naturespath.com/en-us/recipes/pumped-muesli-chia-pudding/

Nava. (2013, June 17). *Quinoa Breakfast Bowl*. VegKitchen. https://www.vegkitchen.com/quinoa-breakfast-bowl/

Olsen, N. (2018, February 19). *Gluten-free diet: Foods, benefits, and risks*. Medical News Today. https://www.medicalnewstoday.com/articles/288406

Paleo Leap. (2018, May 30). *11 Ways Gluten Can Damage Your Health*. Paleo Leap. https://paleoleap.com/11-ways-gluten-and-wheat-can-damage-your-health/

Palin, M. (2017, August 22). *Gluten-free Cinnamon Raisin Bagel Chips {Dairy-Free Too}*. My Gluten-Free Kitchen. https://mygluten-freekitchen.com/gluten-free-cinnamon-raisin-bagel-chips-dairy-free-too/

Patalsky, K. (2014, September 12). *Cinnamon Toast Morning Muffins, Gluten-Free and Vegan*. Healthy Happy Life. https://healthyhappylife.com/cinnamon-toast-morning-muffins-gluten/

Pavliv, D. (2012, August 16). *The Gluten-Free Craze: Is It Just a Fad or Is It Necessary?* National Center for Health Research. https://www.center4research.org/gluten-free-craze-just-fad-necessary/#:~:text=Some%20scientists%20have%20suggested%20that

Penner, J. (2018, March 28). *Breakfast Macaroni and Cheese*. Frugal Living Mom. https://www.frugallivingmom.com/breakfast-macaroni-and-cheese/

Piro, J. D. (2020). *Grilled Pork with Avocado Salsa*. Taste of Home. https://www.tasteofhome.com/recipes/grilled-pork-with-avocado-salsa/

Porto, A. (2020, August 27). *Gluten-Free Shopping Tips for Parents*. Healthy Children. https://www.healthychildren.org/English/healthy-living/nutrition/Pages/Gluten-Free-Shopping-Tips-for-Parents.aspx

REFERENCES

Primal Palate. (n.d.). *Breakfast Burrito*. Primal Palate. https://www.primalpalate.com/paleo-recipe/breakfast-burrito/

Renee, J. (2008). *What Are the Benefits of Children Eating Snacks During School?* SF Gate. https://healthyeating.sfgate.com/benefits-children-eating-snacks-during-school-4999.html

Ruder, S. (2020). *Feta Shrimp Skillet*. Taste of Home. https://www.tasteofhome.com/recipes/feta-shrimp-skillet/

Rush University Medical Center. (2019). *The Science Behind Breakfast*. Rush University Medical Center. https://www.rush.edu/health-wellness/discover-health/why-you-should-eat-breakfast

Sakai, J. (2013, September 25). *John Hawks Explores How Celiac Disease Evolved*. University of Wisconsin-Madison. https://news.wisc.edu/john-hawks-explores-how-celiac-disease-evolved/

Sanders, J. (2013, March 11). *10 Surprising Benefits of a Gluten-Free Diet*. Jeff Sanders. https://www.jeffsanders.com/benefits-of-a-gluten-free-diet/

Schaefer, A. (2018). *Why Do I Get Tired After Eating? Symptoms of Fatigue*. Healthline. https://www.healthline.com/health/food-nutrition/why-do-i-feel-tired-after-eating

REFERENCES

Schär. (n.d.-a). *Digestion of Gluten.* Dr. Schär Institute. https://www.drschaer.com/us/institute/a/digestion-gluten#:~:text=The%20enzymes%20cleave%20or%20break

Schär. (n.d.-b). *How to Cope with a Celiac Disease Diagnosis | Vida sin gluten.* Dr. Schär Institute. https://www.schaer.com/en-us/a/cope-celiac-disease

Schmidt, D. (2019, September 2). *Gluten-Free Thai Peanut Noodles.* The Spruce Eats. https://www.thespruceeats.com/thai-peanut-noodles-3217109

Shull, M. (2017, October 5). *Gluten-Free Eating: Food and Nutrition Tips for Your Child.* Nationwide Childrens. https://www.nationwidechildrens.org/family-resources-education/700childrens/2017/10/gluten-free-eating-food-and-nutrition-tips-for-your-child

SkinnyMs. (2013, January 8). *Quick & Easy Sweet Potato Crunchies.* Skinny Ms. https://skinnyms.com/sweet-potato-crunchies/

Smith, J. (2018). *What is Gluten?* Celiac Disease Foundation. https://celiac.org/gluten-free-living/what-is-gluten/

Steen, J. (2016, July 11). Breakfast Can Set You Up For A Happier, Positive Day. *Huffington Post.* https://www.huffingtonpost.com.au/2016/07/10/breakfast-can-set-you-up-for-a-happier-positive-day_a_21429436/

REFERENCES

Stone, J. J. (2014, May 18). *Breakfast Pizza with Gluten-Free Cauliflower Crust*. Jerry James Stone. https://jerryjamesstone.com/recipe/breakfast-pizza-with-gluten-free-cauliflower-crust/

Strawbridge, H. (2018, January 8). *Going Gluten-Free Just Because? Here's What You Need to Know*. Harvard Health Blog. https://www.health.harvard.edu/blog/going-gluten-free-just-because-heres-what-you-need-to-know-201302205916

Sundblad, D. (n.d.). *Is Celiac Disease Hereditary?* LoveToKnow. Retrieved October 8, 2020, from https://gluten.lovetoknow.com/celiac-disease/is-celiac-disease-hereditary

The Difference Between Celiac Disease, Gluten Intolerance, and Wheat Allergy | CTG Blog. (2018, June 21). Closing the Gap. https://www.closingthegap.ca/the-difference-between-celiac-disease-gluten-intolerance-and-wheat-allergy/#:~:text=When%20a%20celiac%20person%20ingests

Tidwell, K. (2019). *Why Eating on a Schedule May Improve Your Digestion*. Stop Colon Cancer Now. https://www.stopcoloncancernow.com/buttseriously/healthy-living-tips/why-eating-on-a-schedule-may-improve-your-digestion

REFERENCES

Turea, M. (2020, February 7). *4 Dangers Of A Gluten Free Diet If You Are Not Celiac*. I'm Aware. https://www.imaware.health/blog/risks-of-a-gluten-free-diet

UChicago Medicine. (n.d.). *Frequently Asked Questions*. Cure Celiac Disease. https://www.cureceliacdisease.org/faq/what-other-autoimmune-disorders-are-typically-associated-with-those-who-have-celiac-disease/

UChicago Medicine. (2020). *Treatment of Celiac Disease*. Cure Celiac Disease. https://www.cureceliacdisease.org/treatment/#:~:text=The%20only%20treatment%20for%20celiac

Watson, S. (2015). *Autoimmune Diseases: Types, Symptoms, Causes and More*. Healthline. https://www.healthline.com/health/autoimmune-disorders

WebMD. (2017, January 5). *What Are the Treatments for Celiac Disease?* WebMD. https://www.webmd.com/digestive-disorders/celiac-disease/celiac-disease-treatment#1

Whitby, K. (2014, February 21). *No-Crust Pizza Bites: Gluten Free, Low Carb*. Ella Claire & Co. https://www.ellaclaireinspired.com/no-crust-pizza-bites/

Whiteman, H. (2016, September 6). *Gluten-Free Diet Gains Popularity, Despite No Rise in Celiac Disease*.

REFERENCES

Medical News Today. https://www.medicalnewstoday.com/articles/312723

Wielgus, M. (2020). *Easy Cuban Picadillo*. Taste of Home. https://www.tasteofhome.com/recipes/easy-cuban-picadillo/

Williams, M.-J. (2013, February 20). *Advice for going gluten-free with kids*. Washington Post. https://www.washingtonpost.com/lifestyle/on-parenting/advice-for-going-gluten-free-with-kids/2013/02/19/66fa1534-722c-11e2-a050-b83a7b35c4b5_story.html

Wolford, D. (2020). *7 Signs Your Child is Gluten Intolerant*. Weed 'em & Reap. https://www.weedemandreap.com/7-signs-child-gluten-intolerant/

Wright, L. (2012, March 29). *Banana Coconut Waffles*. The First Mess. https://thefirstmess.com/2012/03/29/banana-coconut-waffles/

IMAGE REFERENCES

All images have been sourced from https://unsplash.com

Figure 1: Child. From Unsplash, by Rusty Watson, 2020. https://unsplash.com/photos/xh77Hx9Im2s

REFERENCES

Figure 2: Celiac. From Unsplash, by Janko Ferlič, 2017. https://unsplash.com/photos/oWDRVgk04EA

Figure 3: The Gluten-Free Diet. From Unsplash, by Anna Pelzer, 2017. https://unsplash.com/photos/IGfIGP5ONV0

Figure 4: Empower Your Child. From Unsplash, by Nathan Dumlao, 2020. https://unsplash.com/photos/ns1xhGumyH8

Figure 5: Breakfast. From Unsplash, by Brooke Lark, 2017. https://unsplash.com/photos/W9OKrxBqiZA

Figure 6: Smoothie Bowl. From Unsplash, by Aneta Pawlik, 2020. https://unsplash.com/photos/QsAbKuVL1Fw

Figure 7: Mac & Cheese. From Unsplash, by Hermes Rivera, 2018. https://unsplash.com/photos/7ld9_oZDdQs

Figure 8: Choco Chip Pancakes. From Unsplash, by Tosca Olivi, 2020. https://unsplash.com/photos/trt7eH46oRA

Figure 9: Banana Waffles. From Unsplash, by Alena Ganzheia, 2020. https://unsplash.com/photos/AFFbJzJcXdw

Figure 10: Snacks. From Unsplash, by S'well, 2019. https://unsplash.com/photos/ESY-Nupt170

Figure 11: Chocolate Pudding. From Unsplash, by American Heritage Chocolate, 2020. https://unsplash.com/photos/RQ4TXxFaaZc

REFERENCES

Figure 12: Healthy Parfait. From Unsplash, by amirali mirhashemian, 2019. https://unsplash.com/photos/W2d_FskKkpw

Figure 13: Brownies. From Unsplash, by dapiki moto, 2020. https://unsplash.com/photos/pRdAzONlxqc

Figure 14: Chia Pudding. From Unsplash, by Kaffee Meister, 2019. https://unsplash.com/photos/QejPtWZOMjI

Figure 15: Lunch. From Unsplash, by Ella Olsson, 2018. https://unsplash.com/photos/4dQiaWKiL-Y

Figure 16: Rainbow Rice Bowl. From Unsplash, by Food Photographer David Fedulov, 2020. https://unsplash.com/photos/zhkhwGrqilw

Figure 17: Classic Spaghetti. From Unsplash, by Danijela Prijovic, 2020. https://unsplash.com/photos/qits91IZv1o

Figure 18: Beef Tacos. From Unsplash, by Tai's Captures, 2019. https://unsplash.com/photos/JiRSy0GfqPA

Figure 19: Vegetable Soup. From Unsplash, by Ella Olsson, 2019. https://unsplash.com/photos/fxJTl_gDh28

Figure 20: Happy Kid. From Unsplash, by Sharon McCutcheon, 2018. https://unsplash.com/photos/df106IZ5Hck